LAND
without
BORDERS

LAND

without

BORDERS

How God Guides You
through the Wilderness

JOHN A. BECK

Discovery House.
from Our Daily Bread Ministries

Discovery House is affiliated with Our Daily Bread
Ministries, Grand Rapids, Michigan.

Requests for permission to quote from this book should be directed
to: Permissions Department, Discovery House, PO Box 3566, Grand
Rapids, MI 49501, or contact us by email at permissionsdept@dhp.org.

ISBN: 978-1-62707-884-9

Printed in the United States of America

First printing in 2018

For Aaron, Peter, Jonathan, Jared, Jacob, and Hannah.
The Lord is our Shepherd in every season of wilderness.

CONTENTS

Introduction   9

1. Why Geography?   15
2. Why Wilderness?   23
3. What Is Wilderness?   31
4. How Does God Use Wilderness?   45
5. Wilderness and Faith Witness   57
6. Wilderness without Wanting   69
7. Wilderness and Forgiveness   83
8. Wilderness and Extravagant Love for Our Neighbor   95

Appendix: The Bible's Wilderness Vocabulary   107
Notes   125
Land without Borders Video Study Guide   127

INTRODUCTION

EVEN IF YOU HAVE NEVER camped in a remote backcountry setting or bounced your truck along a rugged four-wheel-drive trail, you have likely entered the wilderness. You have visited this land without borders as a Bible reader, because its authors and poets regularly take us there.

Have you noticed? What do you know about this ecosystem? How is it like (or different from) the wildernesses you know from personal experience? Many Bible readers have not thought about questions like these, but they are important—both to our understanding of the biblical accounts and to our own journeys through what I call "seasons of wilderness."

Together, let's explore this idea of wilderness in the Bible. And let's consider how this ecosystem, so often the setting for Bible passages, helps to deliver God's thoughts to us. We are off to this land without borders to see how God guides us through the wilderness.

As we begin the journey, let me tell you why I wrote this book—and why I think it is important for you to read it.

Why I Wrote this Book

I love the solitude of a high mountain trail. I love meeting the plants and trees that call the backcountry their home. I love the bugling of a bull elk and the way my heart races when a grizzly bear crosses my trail. I love the smell of the tundra on a summer afternoon and the taste of my coffee as the first rays of the sun awaken the mountain peaks. In short, I love the wilderness.

I am convinced that my affection for wild nature is no accident. Carefully managed experiences from the early years of my life shaped my thinking about wilderness and prepared me to write this book. Mine is a story of farm life, mountain vacations, and the national conversation about wilderness that accompanied both.

My grandparents had a dairy farm in Lebanon, Wisconsin. Here I learned to drive a tractor, milk a cow, and appreciate the wonders of the created world. Farm life has a way of engendering a love for nature—I see it in two other men who spent time on Wisconsin farms, John Muir and Aldo Leopold. Both wrote powerfully about the idea of wilderness, and I resonate with the way they spoke.

Muir, the father of our national park system, said, "In every walk with nature one receives far more than he seeks."[1] On another occasion, he wrote, "Climb the mountains and get their good tidings. Nature's peace will flow into you as sunshine flows into trees. The winds will blow their freshness into you, and the storms their energy, while cares drop away from you like autumn leaves."[2]

Leopold, a University of Wisconsin faculty member and the father of wildlife ecology, wrote, "We abuse land because we regard it as a commodity belonging to us. When we see land as a community to which we belong, we may begin to use it with love and respect."[3] As I worked on my grandparents' farm, I came to see myself in exactly this way: I am not a master so much as a member of the community of living things.

Summer days not spent on the farm were family vacation time. Each year my family packed the station wagon and traveled to the Rocky Mountains of the American West. The plan for these days was simple: pack everything needed for the journey and wander as deeply as possible into the mountain backcountry.

The string of these summer trips to the American West was broken only twice to make room for extended trips to Alaska. These took place before the Alaska Highway was paved, which meant driving more than thirteen hundred miles of dusty, gravel road that plunged us deeply into the wilds of America's last frontier. Those vacations further certified my love for the wilderness.

The formative years of my youth were also years in which a national conversation—over the very wild places I was coming to love—was stirring. In the 1960s and 70s, America was engaging in a great national debate about the wilderness and its value. This animated discussion indicates that many Americans were beginning to see wilderness very differently than those who first came to our shores.

Imagine if I had grown up during America's Puritan era. The Puritans characterized their efforts to settle the new world as a spiritual battle, one that waged war against the wilderness. For them the wilderness was not only a threatening but an "ungodly" place.[4] And had I lived at the time the first American pioneers moved west, I would have heard wilderness characterized as useless space, a geographic obstacle to the advance of society.

President Andrew Jackson captured this sentiment in a speech in the early nineteenth century. "What good man would prefer a country covered by forests and ranged by a few thousand savages to our extensive Republic, studded with cities, towns, and prosperous farms, embellished with all the improvements which art can devise or industry execute?"[5] In its earliest days, Americans had a passion to civilize wilderness rather than preserve it.

But by the close of the nineteenth century, a different tone was struck. Henry David Thoreau was describing wilderness as a place to discover a meaning-filled life, a place that led mortals to contemplate deep spiritual truths. In 1851, he gave a speech that encouraged Americans to rethink their negative view of wilderness, closing with the words, "in Wildness is the preservation of the World."[6] Many Americans rallied to the cause of wilderness, their thoughts turning to its preservation rather than its eradication. Those who agreed with Thoreau's perspective called for large tracts of the quickly-disappearing wilderness to be set aside, a land deposit on which future generations of Americans like me could draw.

Early in the twentieth century, a new voice—one that had a Christian tone—was raised in support of wilderness preservation. John Muir observed that the faith he had learned in his home was enhanced by his experiences in wild nature. Although God's glory was evident in all his works, Muir concluded that "in wilderness the letters were capitalized."[7] Many Americans agreed.

When I was eight years old, congress passed the Wilderness Protection Act of 1964, setting aside land in its most pristine form—without roads or permanent structures—so that visitors could see nature untarnished by civilization. A fully developed philosophy of wilderness followed, one popularized in books I read, such as Lois Crisler's *Arctic Wild* and Robert Marshall's *Alaska Wilderness*. It was further popularized in the magazines to which our family subscribed: *Backpacker, Outside*, and *Alaska: The Magazine of Life on the Last Frontier*.

Farm life, my travels in the American West, and the national conversation on wilderness are the trails of my youth that led me to where I am now—and to the writing of this book. As a Bible reader who already loved the wilderness, I was drawn to the idea of wilderness mentioned so frequently in the pages of Scripture. In time, I studied this ecosystem as a scholar, ultimately sharing what I learned with my students. As a faculty member and field instructor with Jerusalem University College, I have the great privilege of walking throughout the Promised Land, including its amazing wilderness areas.

On these field trips, my students and I discuss the nature of biblical wilderness and how God used it to shape his people of the past. And we talk about how the Holy Spirit has used this unique ecosystem to deliver some of the most powerful messages we own in the Bible. *Land without Borders* is an opportunity for you to walk these trails with me and listen in on the conversation.

Why You Need to Read This Book

Still not convinced? That may be because you do not share my love for wilderness or, for that matter, a love of the outdoors. So why should you read on?

The wilderness is mentioned hundreds of times in the Bible, so God must have some purpose in taking us to this ecosystem so often. I believe part of that purpose is to help us through our own seasons of wilderness, those difficult times of life when we struggle with relationships, health, finances, or any of the other issues of life that cause us stress.

How can I be sure to get all the comfort and encouragement the Lord has put in those passages? The more I know about this ecosystem, the better I will understand each of those references and the thoughts of God they convey. As you will see in the chapters that follow, wilderness hosts some of the best-known and most-loved portions of God's Word, stories and poetry that will suffer if we read them without considering their wilderness setting.

If you read on, this book will provide insights into the physical nature of biblical wilderness—so when the authors and poets of the Bible mention it, your picture of wilderness will synchronize with theirs. You will come to understand how people in Bible times thought about wilderness and the cultural roles the wilderness played in their lives.

I love the wilderness. And that is no accident. The Lord configured my life so that I might cherish what this ecosystem is and offers—it rightly deserves its place among our national treasures.

But God had a higher purpose in mind: the Lord carefully shaped my life so that I would be drawn to the idea of wilderness in the Bible, intending for me to study and share what I have learned with you. This land without borders has powerful lessons to teach, particularly when our lives enter those "seasons of wilderness." Wilderness stories and poetry reveal why the Lord allows our lives to experience these difficult times, how he supports us during them, and how he can use these wilderness moments to change us for the better.

Wilderness is a land without borders—but not a land without powerful application in our lives.

1

WHY GEOGRAPHY?

BEFORE WE DIVE MORE DEEPLY into a study of biblical wilderness, let's pay a brief visit to the neighborhood in which it lives.

Our study resides within a larger family of research called biblical geography. People like me, the researchers and scholars who specialize in the field, work to familiarize ourselves (and others) with the Bible's physical world, contemplating its impact on our reading of Scripture. An understanding of geography is critical for Bible readers because, unlike other ancient Near Eastern documents, Scripture is filled with place references. In fact, a great deal of what the Lord says to us through the biblical authors and poets has a geographical connection.

After more than twenty-five years of study, it is difficult for me to find a single page in the Bible where this geographical influence is not at work. So, before we narrow our focus to the wilderness, let's dedicate a few pages to explaining the relationship between geography and Scripture. I will assert that the study of geography belongs in the company of Bible study.

Geography and the Human Experience

Let's start with the human experience we all share: we are people of place. Think about that for a moment. Who we are, how we think, and how we naturally communicate with one another is shaped by where we come from.

For example, I live in Wisconsin, just west of Lake Michigan. This geographical reality impacts what I have in my garage, and lies behind some of the expressions I use when I talk about my life here.

In my garage, you will find both a snowblower and a lawn mower, tools that do very different jobs. You may have one or the other, or you may have neither. But I need both because the latitude at which I live requires the use of one during the summer months and the other during the winter. This is geographically determined.

Geography also influences the way I speak. I am reminded of this every time someone says to me, "You sound like someone who lives in Wisconsin." In fact, I do. Let me give you a couple of examples: during the winter months, I speak about "lake effect snow" and during the summer I say it's "cooler by the lake." You may not be familiar with either expression. But living near Lake Michigan, I need language to speak about both natural phenomena.

During the winter months, when the winds are out of the east, moist air over the lake is blown over the much colder land—and that turns this moisture into snow. This phenomenon can quickly produce more than a foot of snow, so its gets its own label: "lake effect." In the summer, an onshore wind brings the cool air above the lake inland, producing a form of natural air-conditioning. So the forecast often calls for summer temperatures that are "cooler by the lake." These are expressions that have a geographic backstory, and when I use language like this, I betray my southeastern Wisconsin heritage.

In the same way, the biblical authors were people of place. Who they were, how they thought, and how they naturally communicated has a relationship to where they were from. They did not have garages with snowblowers and lawn mowers, but they spoke about other devices shaped to meet their geographic realities—tools like olive crushing presses and oil lamps. And, like me, they used local expressions that had a link to land. They spoke about "going up to Jerusalem" and about a "west wind" that created weather very different from that associated with an "east wind."

Geography in the Bible

Did those habits of thought and word find their way into the Bible when the Lord used human writers to communicate his thoughts? Consider what the Bible says about its own origins: "Above all, you must understand that no prophecy of Scripture came about by the prophet's own interpretation of things. For prophecy never had its origin in the human will, but prophets, *though human*, spoke from God as they were carried along by the Holy Spirit" (2 Peter 1:20–21, emphasis mine).

These words describe poets and authors who compose very differently than someone like me. The Holy Spirit influenced what they remembered, sharpened what they recalled, and shaped how they applied those recollections to our lives. With a miracle we cannot fully understand, the Lord superintended the process to make sure that what we have in the Bible is the untarnished Word of God.

But there is another thought tucked into these verses, one that is easy to miss. These unique authors and poets never stopped being themselves. Note the phrase "though human" in the language from 2 Peter above.

What does that mean? The Holy Spirit used the native languages of these inspired authors. He moved them to write in the vocabulary and grammar of their normal, everyday conversations. And he also used the geographical expressions they would have spoken to family members and friends. As the Holy Spirit shared the thoughts of God through these mortals, he never allowed what they wrote to assert something that was not true. He removed the error, but he did not remove the human experience. And because he did not remove the human experience, he did not remove the influence and mention of geography. That is why there is geography in our Bibles. And that is why some of what the Lord says to us in his Word is said using geography.

The Challenge and the Opportunity

The Bible is full of people we recognize and places we don't. It is filled with familiar stories in which we meet unfamiliar places. The biblical authors do not speak like someone "from around here"— or, to put it differently, we don't listen to the biblical authors like someone who is "from around there." And this creates a challenge for us. We may either miss or misunderstand something the Lord is saying in his Word because we may miss or misunderstand the geography he is using to say it.

So what can we do about that? The communication of the Bible is set. We cannot ask for a rewrite that shifts the language of the Bible closer to the geography we know. We can, however, move ourselves in the direction of the biblical authors. We can come to a better understanding of the geography of their world.

Once we have made that commitment, we need to determine exactly what we mean by *geography*. Ask around, and you will find that geography means different things to different people. For some, it's about maps. For others, geography refers to the "lay of the land" (or *topography*). But the world of geographical study is much bigger than just that—it consists of three general parts.

Let's start with "physical geography." This is the study of features on the surface of the earth and the forces that act on them. So geographical study considers things like geology, topography, nature's water systems, weather, and seismic events.

Now, add "human geography" to the mix. Human geography studies the ways in which human experience is shaped by physical geography—and the ways in which humans reshape physical geography. Our study of biblical geography primarily considers the former, which means examining the way people respond to where they live. It considers the kind of food they grow and the tools they use to plant and harvest and process their food. It studies how people get their water, where and how they travel, and the names that they give to places.

Finally, to physical and human geography, we add natural history. Natural history studies the living things on the surface of the earth. It considers the animals, trees, and plants that share the space with us and impact our daily living. As you can see, "geography" covers lots of ground!

Why are these aspects of the Bible so easy to overlook? Part of the answer lies in the fact that the geography of the biblical world is unfamiliar to us. As readers, we are generally prone to skip over things we don't fully understand, making sense of a sentence without taking the missing elements into account. We often do that with geography in the Bible.

On the other hand, we can take something we don't understand and try to make it more familiar to us. In that regard, I may presume that a mountain in the Bible is like a mountain I know. I might assume that the appearance and behavior of the Bible's Jordan River are the same as the Mississippi's. But that is not necessarily the case. I may assign an appearance or some other quality to a piece of biblical geography that is quite unlike the reality known to the author.

We may also fail to notice the geography in the Bible because we have assigned it to the category of trivia. While it is true that there are "Bible trivia games," I would argue that Bible geography is *not* trivial. As the biblical authors and poets turned events into stories and composed their thoughts with poetic verse, the Holy Spirit eliminated all unnecessary detail. We have just those particulars from an event and just those carefully selected words in a poem that are required—just what is essential to communicate the fullness of what the Lord is anxious to say to us.

The breadth of geographical study and our propensity to read past the geography in the Bible can challenge us. But this also presents us with an opportunity.

As modern Bible readers, we have access to tools and experiences that will carry us back and help us better understand the physical geography, human geography, and natural history of the biblical world. As a start, consider reading the booklet *The Lands of the Bible: Places that Shape Scripture*, published in the Discovery Series by Our Daily Bread Ministries. In this booklet, I speak a bit more about what geography is, and I offer thoughts on how people can include geography in their reading of the Bible.

It is also a book that tells more of my story. I was not born a biblical geographer—I experienced a "geographic conversion" in my Bible reading, so I know something about the journey. And after teaching more than two thousand Christian students on field trips in Israel, offering seminars on this topic around the world, and receiving feedback from readers, I can say without hesitation that this is one of the most rewarding things Bible readers can do. When we study the lands of the Bible, we find that our Bible is very much at home *here*. And we'll find ourselves more at home in our own Bibles.

———————————— Review and Reflection ————————————

1. Consider the effect that geography has on you. How does where you live impact your lifestyle? How does your personal geography shape the things you say?

2. Why is there geography in the Bible?

3. The study of geography falls into three categories: physical geography, human geography, and natural history. Define each of these dimensions, and then find Bible passages that illustrate them at work.

4. Geographical elements have always been in your Bible. What has been your typical response as you've come across them?

5. Read Psalm 125:1–2. Identify the words and phrases in these verses that are geographical in nature.

2

WHY WILDERNESS?

SUSAN LOVED HER BIBLE AND had always wanted to visit the Holy Land. Her one and only visit finally took place the month after her retirement. Anxious to get a look at the land, she had already formed a picture in her mind of what she would see.

But that would have to wait, at least for a few days. Susan's group flew in at night, so when I accompanied them to Jerusalem, it was hard to make out much of anything in the moonlight. The first two days in Jerusalem were special, as they are for all Christian pilgrims to this land. But Susan wanted to get beyond the city itself, "to see the land as Sarah and Ruth saw it." That had to wait until the third day, when we left Jerusalem. As we wandered into the countryside, the curtain on the land was pulled back. "Oh, my!" she exclaimed, "This is *nothing* like Texas—*nothing* like I thought it would be!"

Susan's experience is not unique. Nearly all first-time visitors to Israel are shocked by how different its geography is from what they expected. They often assume it will be much more like home than it is. In addition, they are taken aback by this land's diversity. They expect Israel's geography to be uniform when in reality it is a place that changes quickly over short distances.

As Bible readers, we could explore any of the Promised Land's ecosystems and find insights that advance our understanding of God's Word. For example, we could investigate the steeply-sided mountains of Judah's hill country and the verses associated with them. We could study the sprawling Jezreel Valley and its role in Bible history. And then there is the shoreline of the Sea of Galilee, a location filled with stories about Jesus. Given the options available to us, we need to ask, why wilderness?

The question seems even more apropos given that many people today find the very idea of wilderness objectionable. So this question requires a moment of our time: Why, given all the other options, should I study biblical wilderness?

A Shunned Ecosystem

When the first Europeans landed on the shores of what would become America, they saw wilderness differently than the people who already lived here. Native Americans cherished wilderness as a place of provision and spiritual insight. The "new" Americans saw wilderness as a problem that needed to be fixed. "It was instinctively understood as something alien to man," Roderick Frazier Nash writes in *Wilderness and the American Mind*, "an insecure and uncomfortable environment against which civilization had waged an unceasing struggle."[1] There may well be something about wilderness that makes you recoil, both as a person and as a Bible reader. Let's consider why that is the case.

The idea of "wild" resides in the term *wilderness*. For me, I must confess that is part of the appeal. I love wilderness because it is an untamed place, offering adventure, risk, and challenge in ways that a suburban home and a neatly manicured lawn do not. But it is those very traits of wilderness which may make it less appealing to others. If you prefer the security and comfort of urban living—and find the idea of a hiking a backcountry trail or camping in an untamed natural setting unnerving—you may shun not just being in the wilderness but the very *idea* of wilderness. If that sounds like you, you're in good company. You see, most people who lived in Bible times were more like you than me. They shared your concerns about wilderness—and most of them avoided it.

You may also feel disinclined to invest in this idea of wilderness because one of the best-known stories in the Bible links it with divine judgment. The story of Sodom and Gomorrah talks about the conversion of fertile, populated land into an empty wasteland.

When Abram and Lot parted company because their herds had grown too large to live together, Lot selected the plain of the Jordan toward a place called Zoar, near Sodom. The Bible goes on to speak of this place in glowing terms—it was "well watered, like the garden of the LORD, like the land of Egypt" (Genesis 13:10). But the people who lived on this land did not receive such a favorable review.

Lot elected to live among wicked people. Just how wicked becomes clear when we listen in on a conversation between Abram and the Lord. God was planning to destroy Sodom and Gomorrah for their sin, but Abram pressed him to spare the cities if merely ten righteous people could be found within them (Genesis 18:32). The Lord looked but could not find even that many righteous people, so the fate of Sodom and Gomorrah was sealed. Their sin was so egregious that it compelled the kind of divine action we rarely read about in the Bible, an act of judgment so substantial that it not only destroyed the cities but completely changed the surrounding ecosystem. When judgment fell, even the vegetation was eliminated, and good land became a wasteland (Genesis 19:25).

This dramatic change left a lesson on the landscape. Those who physically walked by recalled the divine judgment—and those who visit this wasteland today, as Bible readers, are similarly challenged to recall the story. For example, Moses sternly warned Israel that if they abandoned the Lord, the Promised Land would become a wasteland: "The whole land will be a burning waste of salt and sulfur—nothing planted, nothing sprouting, no vegetation growing on it. It will be like the destruction of Sodom and Gomorrah, Admah and Zeboyim, which the LORD overthrew in fierce anger" (Deuteronomy 29:23). This searing image surfaces again and again in later prophetic warnings: those who abandon the Lord will face the same fate as the people living in Sodom and Gomorrah. Their fertile land will become uninhabitable wilderness (Isaiah 13:19; Jeremiah 23:14, 49:18, 50:40; Amos 4:11).

For various reasons, many people resist the study of biblical wilderness. But that is a most unfortunate choice. Let's consider

reasons for embracing a study of wilderness and the Bible communication linked to it.

An Embraced Ecosystem

Biblical authors and poets mention the wilderness—in one way
or another—more than three hundred times. Left to their own
decision-making, they may not have spoken about this undesirable
ecosystem so often. But it was not their decision. The Holy Spirit
led these people to include the idea of wilderness frequently and
widely in what they wrote.

We find it in both the Old and New Testaments. We encounter
it within the stories as well as in the divinely inspired poetry,
proverbs, and letters of this sacred book. The conclusion is
inescapable: the Lord has chosen to share many of his thoughts
with us through the idea of wilderness. So by enhancing our
understanding of this ecosystem, we will open new insights into
many, many verses of the Bible.

This would be true even if all these passages spoke of divine
judgment or other somber topics. But that is not the case. Some of
the best known, most loved, most reassuring passages in the Bible
flow from experiences in the wilderness, using imagery from the
wilderness. Good or bad, happy or sad, all of these stories have
something to teach us.

We can learn much from the longest wilderness story told in the
Bible. When the Lord brought Israel out of Egypt, he did not lead
them directly to the Promised Land as we might expect. Instead
he led them into the wilderness, where they remained for *forty
years*. Clearly, God had a purpose in this extended wilderness
stay, a purpose we will consider in chapter 4.

Centuries after this time in the wilderness, Israel formed a
kingdom—this is the era in which the Lord anointed David to
succeed Saul, the first king, who failed to be the kind of leader
the Lord wanted for his people. Saul was not ready to give up his
title, though, so he tried to take David's life. David fled into the

wilderness, where he remained for years, using this ecosystem for sustenance and shelter from the murderous hand of Saul. It was an austere place for the future king of Israel to live, but the Lord used that austerity to shape David's faith and character—he would become the kind of leader the Lord wanted.

And David's descendant Jesus spent time in the wilderness. Like Israel, Jesus was led by a divine hand into the wilderness for a time of testing. The full sense of what he experienced and how he was using this ecosystem to teach important spiritual lessons depends on our acquaintance with this space.

There are positive, even uplifting, wilderness stories that are meant to bring us comfort, direction, and hope. But we will only extract all they offer when we read them as wilderness stories.

And, as I've already noted, these stories are particularly suited to address the seasons of wilderness we experience in life. Yes, that is right: wilderness is not just an ecosystem, but also a season of life. You may not have used that language before, but consider what such difficult times of life have in common with wilderness.

Some experiences leave us feeling lost, vulnerable, unempowered, helpless, threatened, overwhelmed, discouraged, and isolated. These wilderness seasons of life come in many shapes and sizes, including broken relationships, illnesses, accidents, loss of employment, financial reversals, natural disasters, and the deaths of those nearest and dearest to us. Although everyone's situation is unique, all of us have this in common: during the most difficult seasons of life, we experience the same feelings and faith challenges that exist in a physical wilderness. Both cause us to feel the full weight of our own limitations. Hope is hard to come by. No matter which way we look we see realities that loom larger than our native abilities. These circumstances make it clear that what we have to bring to the challenge is not enough. This is a season of wilderness.

And here is what I have found to be so powerful—the most compelling reason for engaging the idea of wilderness in the Bible.

These stories speak directly and practically to our own wilderness seasons of life.

In these stories, we see people engaged in experiences that mirror our own. These biblical characters speak authentically about our own worries, doubts, frustrations, and fears. In their lives, we see how God thinks about people in wilderness, how he tests and matures people's faith in the wilderness, how he cares for people in wilderness, how he sustains people in wilderness, and how he restores people by leading them *out* of the wilderness.

If forced to surrender some portion of my Bible, I would fight to keep the wilderness-bound stories. They are particularly apt at providing the comfort, direction, and encouragement we desperately need when our pathway becomes cluttered with the cares of life.

Whether you are deeply immersed in a season of wilderness, know someone who is, or want to prepare yourself for such a time, the road ahead is the same. It is time to enter the biblical wilderness and see what this place is all about.

——————————— Review and Reflection ———————————

1. Does the idea of wilderness attract or repulse you? Why?
2. How does the story about Sodom and Gomorrah shape the way Bible readers may feel about wilderness?
3. Why do you think wilderness is mentioned so often in the Bible?
4. Give your own definition for a "season of wilderness."
5. How do wilderness passages in the Bible address the seasons of wilderness we meet in our lives?

3

WHAT IS WILDERNESS?

EVERYONE WHO KNEW ME AS a kid knew that I was all about the outdoors. I loved being outdoors. I loved playing outside in the woods with my friends, building forts and pretending to ward off imaginary attackers. I loved hunting pheasants in the cornfields of my grandparent's farm. And I particularly loved our family's summer vacations spent in the wilderness areas of the American west. Rambling over the tundra spying on mountain sheep or trekking through the ponderosa pines in search of elk—this was a high point of my year.

Then I went to Sunday school. Don't get me wrong—I loved the stories. But I remember struggling with the story of Israel's extended stay in the wilderness after they had left Egypt. My teacher said it was such a horrible time. How could that be? They were in the wilderness! That is where you go to vacation!

I have since learned that I was not the only one who has misunderstood the wilderness of the biblical world. So before we engage those wilderness stories, let's spend a little time answering questions like these: How did the inspired writers define *wilderness*? What qualities of wilderness stood out most boldly in their minds? What value did they see in wilderness?

Wilderness in America

First, let's acknowledge that our idea of biblical wilderness has been either aided or impaired by our modern notion of wilderness. That notion that has had a long and uneven history in American thought. We will focus on two periods, the beginning and the middle of the twentieth century, when the definition of wilderness was more firmly set in the American mind.

At the close of the nineteenth century, the Wild West had been tamed and the line marking the American frontier erased. Much had been gained for the civilized world. But now people began to ask what America had lost.

How had contact with wilderness shaped the American identity, and what would happen if that contact were lost? What would become of Americans who no longer had wild places to retreat to?

In the end, a consensus was reached: wilderness had value for America at many levels. And if actions were not taken quickly to preserve parcels of wild land, the opportunity to save such places could be lost. This passion for preservation led to the establishment of the first national park, Yellowstone, in 1872, as well as the formation of the Sierra Club (1892) and the Wilderness Society (1935).

Aldo Leopold, who we met in the introduction, argued that land should be set aside within the national forest system and preserved with a new designation. He referred to this special national space as "wilderness," going on to define what he meant by wilderness in an article written for the *Journal of Forestry*. Here is the key sentence. "By 'wilderness' I mean a continuous stretch of country preserved in its natural state, open to lawful hunting and fishing, big enough to absorb a two-weeks' pack trip, and kept devoid of roads, artificial trails, cottages, or other works of man."[1] To Leopold, size was critical—if all the lifeforms were to persist in their natural state, designated wilderness areas would require large expanses of land. And unlike national parks and national forests, Leopold proposed that wilderness areas remain free of commercial development, receiving the barest minimum of human improvement.

Americans debated the value of Leopold's definition and the idea of Americans co-owning large tracts of wilderness. A national discussion followed and in the end affirmed the value of wild places: Congress passed the Wilderness Protection Act of 1964. It contained this definition of wilderness: "A wilderness, in contrast to those areas where man and his own works dominate the landscape, is hereby recognized as an area where the earth and its life are untrammeled by man, where man himself is a visitor who does not remain. An area of wilderness is further defined to mean in this Act an area of undeveloped Federal land retaining its primeval character and influence, without permanent improvements or human habitation."[2] Guided by this definition, the federal government began to set aside thousands of acres of land. Today nearly 5 percent of America is federally designated wilderness, including areas as different from one another as the Boundary Waters Canoe Area in Minnesota, the John Muir Wilderness in the California Sierras, and the Okefenokee Wilderness in Georgia.

As an American, this is how I have been taught to think about wilderness. It is a place where nature is unrestrained, unchanged by modern interventions. Wilderness areas include Western mountain tundra, Eastern forests, Midwestern lakes, Southwestern deserts, and Southeastern swampland. And that brings us to this critical question: From this picture, what can I use to shape my impressions of biblical wilderness?

Wilderness in the Bible

For our culture, modern American history has favored us with a definition of wilderness. Unfortunately, we don't have something like this in the biblical literature—it mentions but does not formally define what it means by wilderness. So we have to discover how people in Bible times thought about wilderness. To do so, we can examine the terms they used for this ecosystem and the actual physical qualities of the areas they knew as wilderness. Considering this evidence, we can deduce several qualities of biblical wilderness.

Biblical writers used twelve different terms—ten in the Old Testament, two in the New—to refer to the region we are studying. This vocabulary includes both general terms for the idea of wilderness and more specific terms that highlight the distinct qualities of wilderness. (I have included an appendix, "The Bible's Wilderness Vocabulary," that you can use to trace the usage of those terms throughout the Bible.)

As English Bible readers, we meet these words in translation. The idea of wilderness is expressed in terms like *wilderness, desert, desolate place, wasteland, dry place, parched ground, deserted place,* and *remote place.* These terms give us an impression of how people in Bible times thought about this ecosystem.

We also get a sense of what came to their minds when we look at the common qualities of the regions that the biblical authors designate as "wilderness." These include the Wilderness of Beersheba (Genesis 21:14), the Wilderness of Shur (Exodus 15:22), the Wilderness of Sin (Exodus 17:1), the Wilderness of Sinai (Leviticus 7:38), the Wilderness of Paran (Numbers 10:12), the Desert of Judah (Judges 1:16; or "wilderness of Judea," Matthew 3:1), the Wilderness of Ziph (1 Samuel 23:14), the Wilderness of En Gedi (1 Samuel 24:1), the Wilderness of Jeruel (2 Chronicles 20:16), and the Wilderness of Tekoa (2 Chronicles 20:20).

These regions vary from one another in terms of rainfall, geology, and topography. Some of these areas are arid, sandy deserts while others are steppe land, dry basins, or even towering granite mountains. But we can tighten our frame of reference by focusing on the wilderness regions that had the greatest impact on the biblical authors and poets. These are places where the story of the Bible has the longest and most frequent connection with wilderness—the Wilderness of Sinai, the Wilderness of Zin, and the Wilderness of Judea.

When we consider the natural realities that these regions have in common, we are left with seven key qualities of biblical wilderness. These are the qualities that will prove most helpful in synching our understanding of wilderness with that of the biblical writers.

1. *Wilderness is vast and rugged.*

   Over the years, I have introduced many people to wilderness areas of the Bible by literally walking within them. When I have asked for first impressions, two responses stand out above all the others: vast and rugged.

Let's start with vast. While some regions in the Promised Land are rather small, easily viewed from one location, wilderness reaches to and over the horizon. It is expansive, capable of filling hundreds of square miles.

But wilderness is not only vast; it is remarkably rugged. If we are not standing in the mountains, then mountains are in view. The prophet Jeremiah described the wilderness through which Israel walked on the way to the Promised Land as a "land of deserts and ravines" (2:6). Flat desert stretches give way to deeply cut valleys and mountainous terrain.

First impressions are important. Here is one: wilderness is vast and rugged.

2. *Wilderness is a land with little water.*

All living things need water, and wilderness has precious little of it. Of all the ways in which biblical authors and poets describe this land, they most frequently make the point that it is a place without water. Consider these examples from Isaiah and Jeremiah: Wilderness is a "parched land" and a "sun-scorched land" (Isaiah 35:1; 58:11). It is a "land of drought," "a dry land," and a "desert" (Jeremiah 2:6; 50:12).

The absence of water in the Bible's wilderness areas is related to two factors: distance from the Mediterranean Sea and the presence of a mountain range between the sea and wilderness. The Mediterranean Sea fills the Middle Eastern air with moisture that makes landfall after the wind blows it eastward. The farther inland you go, the less water is left in the air mass to produce rainfall or dew. So we tend to find wilderness areas many miles inland from the Mediterranean.

But mountain ranges also play a role. They are roadblocks for moisture, lifting and cooling moist air masses, extracting their rainfall on their western slopes at the expense of land to the east. Geographers describe this phenomenon with the term "rainfall shadow." This shadow is particularly evident when we consider the annual rainfall totals of Jerusalem and Jericho, which are just fifteen miles apart. Jerusalem, lying just west of watershed line of Israel's central mountain spine, receives twenty-two inches of annual precipitation. Jericho, lying to the east of the watershed line and within the rainfall shadow, receives just six and one-half inches of annual precipitation. Such meager rainfall totals impact the availability of water both on the surface and beneath the ground. As rainfall totals drop, surface watercourses run dry and the subsurface water table drops. The latter means that wells do not recharge and springs fail.

In the Pentateuch, Moses told two stories in which the people of Israel were faced by an interruption in their water supply, one that was resolved only when the Lord miraculously supplied the people's need (Exodus 17:1–7; Numbers 20:1–13). Given the nature of the place and their forty-year stay in the wilderness, these stories are just two examples of what must have been many such miracles required to sustain Israel. Wilderness is a land with precious little water.

3. *Wilderness is a land without grain fields.*

The diet of people in Bible times was dominated by grain and grain products.[3] Heads of grain were eaten raw or roasted to become something like our breakfast cereal. Grain kernels were ground into flour to provide the critical ingredient for the baked goods served at every ancient meal. Only when we realize that grain products accounted for up to one-third of the nutrients of the ancient diet will we appreciate this language from Nehemiah: "We and our sons and daughters are numerous; in order for us to eat and stay alive, we must get grain." (Nehemiah 5:2) To live meant having grain.

But what was most needed was completely lacking in the wilderness. This follows the low rainfall totals I have already mentioned. The most drought-tolerant form of barley available to the ancients required twelve inches of annual precipitation, while the more desirable wheat needed twenty-four inches. That is why people in Bible times tended to distinguish land as that on which grain could be grown and that on which it could not.

Jeremiah looked at the land through which Israel moved on the way to the Promised Land and summed it up as "land not sown" (Jeremiah 2:2). It was the kind of land in which food miracles were necessary for survival; during their forty-year stay in the wilderness, the most regularly reported miracle saw the Lord providing his people with a grain substitute. The substance was not familiar to them, so the Israelites gave it a name that is really a question, calling it *manna* (Hebrew for "what is it?"). The Lord provided this miraculous manna for Israel's entire stay in the wilderness, stopping only when they arrived in the Promised Land, where grain could be raised (Deuteronomy 8:16; Joshua 5:12).

While the people were on the way, Moses was quick to remind them that where they *were* contrasted sharply with where they were *going*. They were traveling toward "a land with wheat and barley" (Deuteronomy 8:8).

4. *Wilderness is land without permanent residents.*

People in Bible times lived where food and water were locally available. The wilderness was not that place. So while there might be military outposts where soldiers were billeted for a time in the wilderness, the casual observer's impression is that wilderness is a place without permanent residents. That is still the case today. Many Bible locations have changed significantly, filling with people, cities, and urban infrastructure, but the wilderness has not. It remains what it was—a "remote place" (Leviticus 16:22).

To be sure, there are place names associated with the wilderness, but don't be fooled into thinking that wilderness was the home to large cities. Take Numbers 33 as an example: the bulk of this chapter consists of a list of places used to define stages in Israel's travel from Egypt to the Promised Land. This list may give you the impression that God's people were traveling from one city to the next, but that is not the case. At best, the places mentioned were wilderness outposts.

Today, some of these locations tell a more detailed story because of the artifacts their former residents left behind. Such places can be identified and placed on a map with greater certainty. But in most cases, Israel's journey is defined with place names that cannot be plotted on a map, because they have no previous or subsequent history and no artifacts to be studied. In most cases, they were not places that had names before Israel arrived—Moses gave them names when the people stopped at each location. Many of these names are descriptive terms that reveal how the place looked to those setting up camp. For example, *Hazeroth* ("green place"), *Rithmah* ("place with broom trees"), and *Libnah* ("white place").

Given the lack of natural resources, wilderness areas struggled to host major cities—but prominent cities could become like wilderness areas. Isaiah used this metaphoric language to characterize a large, fortified city that had suffered defeat in battle: "an abandoned settlement, forsaken like the wilderness" (Isaiah 27:10).

All of that to say when we meet a wilderness story, it will be one that "lives off the grid." At the close of the nineteenth century, George Adam Smith described the Wilderness of Judea with a maritime metaphor that is as true today as it was then—and true of *all* biblical wilderness: "You may travel for hours, and feel as solitary as at sea without a sail in sight."[4] Wilderness is what Jeremiah called it, a "land where no one travels and no one lives" (2:6). Wilderness stories are set in isolation from others because the wilderness is a place without permanent residents.

5. *Wilderness is a land with loosely defined borders.*

Clearly defined borders are necessary when people live close to one another. Being able to define the limits of property holdings goes to practical matters like who owns the land on which a well is dug, a grain field is planted, or a house is built.

When Israel arrived in the Promised Land, the Lord tasked Joshua with dividing it among the twelve tribes of Israel. He used a special procedure that included a written appraisal of the parcels and the casting of lots (at the sanctuary in Shiloh) to assign the parcels to individual tribes (Joshua 18:1–10). And lest a question arise later about the location of tribal boundaries, several chapters in the book of Joshua carefully define those boundary lines (chapters 15–21). But wilderness areas stand in stark contrast to this meticulous definition of borders.

In a place like the wilderness, there was no need for a well-defined border. A land without natural resources and people is not a place where people care about boundaries. Look at a Bible atlas or the maps in the back of your Bible and you will see great wilderness areas identified on the map. What you will not see is hard and fast edges—they just don't exist. Wilderness is a land with loosely defined borders.

6. *Wilderness is a land with very few travelers.*

People traveled through the wilderness only when they had to, because wilderness travel was difficult and dangerous. In fact, virtually all travel in Bible times was difficult and dangerous—read Psalm 121 and you will get a sense for the complications and risks that were part of an ordinary travel day. These difficulties and dangers only increased in the wilderness.

Since wilderness trails were more lightly traveled, the path became less distinct and easier to lose. And the wilderness was no place to get lost. Even where the trail was more easily identified, it was rough. The forms of road maintenance known to Bible-times travelers— straightening, leveling, and removing stones—were typically not done on wilderness trails (Isaiah 40:3–4). They were simply more difficult to walk.

When contemplating a wilderness journey, it was vital to think ahead about provisions and water. During some periods and in some areas, there were caravan stations. However, these were widely scattered, and resupply at such stations was not guaranteed. So it was necessary to plan for and carry food, fodder for pack animals, and medicine to last the entire trip. Finally, and most importantly, people needed to think about hydration. Water stops had to be carefully planned and contingencies considered to account for a source that had dried up.

Wilderness travel was not just difficult, it was also dangerous. A fall could easily result in a turned ankle or broken bone (Psalm 121:3). Under the best of circumstances, this kind of injury would slow the travel pace, increasing the time one was exposed to all the other threats. Travel under the relentless heat of the afternoon sun could easily lead to dehydration (Psalm 121:6). Animals and insects put travelers at risk—Moses spoke about the "venomous snakes and scorpions" that called the wilderness home and impacted the lives of the Israelites during their time in the wilderness (Deuteronomy 8:15). Larger predators also posed a threat (1 Samuel 17:28, 36), as did other human beings who looked to prey on wilderness travelers. Jesus spoke about thieves on the wilderness road between Jericho and Jerusalem, people who beat and robbed a traveler, leaving him for dead (Luke 10:30).

While traveling most roads during Bible times, it was likely you would have company. But that was not true of travel in the wilderness. Given the difficulty and the risks, people used these roads only when necessary. Encountering so few travelers over such a large landscape meant you felt like you were alone. As Jeremiah said, wilderness is a landscape where "no one travels and no one lives" (2:6).

7. *Wilderness is a land that lacks everything.*

Of course, this is an overstatement. Wilderness has many wonderful things to offer. But what it lacks are those things necessary to sustain human life.

Revisit the first six qualities of wilderness that we have noted above. They all speak of a land that is "without" something other places offer. Throughout the Israelites' wilderness stay, the Promised Land toward which they were moving was persistently pictured as a land that offered what the wilderness did not. It was a land "flowing with milk and honey" (Exodus 3:8; Leviticus 20:24; Numbers 14:8; Deuteronomy 6:3). Parts of the Promised Land had such a thriving ecosystem that they were defined as a "land that lacks nothing whatever" (Judges 18:10). By contrast, the wilderness is called "a barren and howling waste" (Deuteronomy 32:10).

George Adam Smith observed that for Judeans living next to wilderness was like "living next door to doom."[5] From the human needs perspective, the wilderness is a land that lacks everything.

The Value of Wilderness

So what value did people in Bible times see in the wilderness? For sure, they did not think about recreation. That is what I personally think about, but I dare not intrude my interests into the reading of wilderness stories in the Bible. I need to see the value of wilderness as these ancient people did.

First, it could be used to pasture animals. Wilderness exists on an ecological continuum from semiarid to fully arid, and the semiarid areas were used as seasonal pasturage for livestock. These were not enduring pastures, but for a few short months during the winter, enough rainfall reached the edges of certain wilderness areas to produce a viable space to graze sheep and goats. Biblical authors mention such wilderness pastures (Psalm 65:12; Jeremiah 23:10; Joel 1:19, 2:22; 1 Samuel 17:28).

Second, wilderness was a place you could go to get away from everyone else. David used the wilderness to escape from Saul (1 Samuel 23:14). But this isolation was also sought by those who needed a quiet place for reflection. It is a space "without" the things and thoughts that distract, so it is a place to ponder. John Muir found wilderness to function in this way: "I only went out for a walk, and finally concluded to stay out until sundown, for going out, I found, was really going in."[6] The Lord led Israel into the wilderness where they stayed for forty years. During that time, he used wilderness experiences to prepare them spiritually before taking them physically into the Promised Land. Similarly, John the Baptist, Jesus, and the apostle Paul made use of the wilderness in advance of entering their public ministries (Luke 1:80, 4:1; Galatians 1:17).

What is wilderness? While some of our impressions of the American wilderness will transfer and prove helpful in reading the biblical texts, others will not. To read the wilderness passages of the Bible well, we need a definition and understanding of the wilderness that matches that of the biblical authors. Now, with those impressions in place, it is time to enter into the longest of Scripture's wilderness stories. We will see how the Lord used the Israelites' time in the wilderness to shape their character and faith.

———————— Reflection and Discussion ————————

1. Before reading this chapter, what was your reaction to the idea of wilderness?

2. How has your reaction to wilderness changed now that you have read this chapter?

3. Where had your perception of wilderness matched the perception of biblical authors?

4. Where had your perception of wilderness diverged significantly from the perception of biblical authors?

5. Read Jeremiah 2:6. This passage comes as close as any to offering a biblical definition of wilderness. List the qualities mentioned that are most helpful in shaping your picture of biblical wilderness.

6. Write a one-sentence definition of biblical wilderness that captures the key nature of this ecosystem.

4

HOW DOES GOD USE WILDERNESS?

THE STORIES IN THE BIBLE and the stories of our lives have this in common: they wander in and out of wilderness.

In the Bible, we walk alongside individuals like Moses, David, John the Baptist, and Jesus. Their stories quite literally move in and out of wildernesses. These experiences were neither fun nor accidental—they were not adventure vacations for those bored with life nor were they the product of poor navigation, mistaken turns on the road to some other place. Many Bible people went to the wilderness intentionally, at the Lord's direction, so they could be honed physically, mentally, spiritually, and emotionally for the roles they would play in the plan of salvation.

But along the way, they asked the same questions we do when our lives enter a season of wilderness. "Why Lord? Why have you led me here? I feel so powerless and threatened—what are you doing?" Of course, there is an answer in the familiar words of Romans 8:28: "We know that in all things God works for the good of those who love him, who have been called according to his purpose." This catchall language includes seasons of wilderness, so we have the assurance that we will be benefited in some way, however undefined. But can we know more about how the Lord intends to use a season of wilderness in our lives?

Yes, we can. But we will need to turn to a portion of the Bible that may be less familiar to us—a chapter that gets considerably less attention than Romans 8. I am speaking of the eighth chapter of Deuteronomy.

Israel's Surprising Separation from the Promised Land

The wilderness is not a place we expect to find Israel, but it is exactly where we find them most often in the Pentateuch.

The first five books of the Old Testament focus our attention on three locations—Canaan, Egypt, and the wilderness—telling the story of Abraham's family. From the start, we expect this story to be a Canaan story, because Canaan is the land linked to a series of promises given to Abram, in the days before God changed his name. The Lord told Abram that his family would grow into a great nation; that they would have Canaan as their own land; and that from this nation, on this land, the Messiah would restore the blessing lost in the garden of Eden (Genesis 12:1–3, 6–7).

But in the very next verses, something surprising happens: Abram leaves Canaan! And although he returns by the start of chapter 13, his departure establishes an unexpected trend in his family's story. Most of it unfolds either in Egypt or in the wilderness.

The extended stay outside the Promised Land begins in Genesis 46. The family of Abraham, under his grandson Jacob, leaves Canaan and travels to Egypt to escape a famine gripping the Promised Land. Given the importance of Canaan to the promises God made to Abraham's family, we expect to find the people quickly back where they belong. But the story of God's chosen people continues in Egypt for dozens of pages . . . and for four hundred years.

This part of the story only makes sense when we go back to God's promises to Abraham, and the way Egypt fostered fulfillment of one of them. This drought-resistant land not only allowed Abraham's family to survive but to thrive, as the Lord used the rich agriculture of Egypt to grow them into a great nation, just as he had promised.

But the political leadership of ancient Egypt did not see things in the same way we do, as readers of Genesis. They felt threatened by the size of this family-turned-nation, so they worked to reduce the numbers by extreme measures—including the killing of every Israelite baby boy. Clearly, it was time for Jacob's family to move on. So the Lord called Moses to lead the chosen people out of Egypt and back to the Promised Land (Exodus 3:8, 17). We would expect them make that return by the quickest route possible.

Again, though, we are surprised by what we read next. Once Israel had safely crossed the Red Sea, God did not turn them north toward the Promised Land but south into the wilderness. The Lord led the people to Mount Sinai, to offer a greater revelation of who he was and who he wanted his people to become. Giving them a detailed code of law, God organized the civil, social, and religious life of this special nation. With that accomplished, Israel was finally on its way to Canaan.

But it is not long before we are surprised again, because the people are turned back at the border. When God's people arrived at the southern edge of Canaan, representatives from each of the Israelite tribes went into Canaan to collect information (Numbers 13:16). The fruit they carried back and the report they offered confirmed everything the Lord had said to Israel about the Promised Land. Joshua and Caleb, two members of that advance team, encouraged the people to seize the moment and enter the land. But the majority of those sent to explore Canaan discouraged the people—they characterized the land as densely populated, bristling with fortifications and menacing warriors.

Rather than dismissing the negative report, the Israelites— showing a remarkable lack of faith, character, and courage—made it their own. Their words provide clear insight into their attitude and plan of action: "If only we had died in Egypt! Or in this wilderness! Why is the LORD bringing us to this land only to let us fall by the sword? Our wives and children will be taken as plunder. Wouldn't it be better for us to go back to Egypt?" (Numbers 14:2–3).

The people hoped for Egypt, but what they got was more wilderness. The Lord turned his chosen people away from the

Promised Land and sent them back into the wilderness, where they would remain for another thirty-eight years. The harsh environment would end the lives of all who participated in the earlier decision not to enter the land (Numbers 14:26–35). Only Joshua and Caleb, along with the next generation of Israelites, would enter the Promised Land.

Genesis led us to expect a Canaan story. But it is not until the opening chapters of Joshua—five books later—that this expectation is fully realized. It had been centuries since Jacob and his family left the land where we expect them to be. Why?

Why Did the Lord Keep Israel in the Wilderness?

Why would the Lord keep his people in the wilderness for such a long time? It must have been a question that surfaced often among those who experienced the extended stay. So just before they left the wilderness to enter the Promised Land, Moses provided the Lord's answer.

We find the explanation in the book of Deuteronomy, written at the very end of Israel's forty years in the wilderness. This book paints the story of Israel's experience with broad brushstrokes, highlighting key events and repeating God's expectations of Israel as a people about to enter the Promised Land.

Deuteronomy 8 captures Moses's words to the assembled Israelites: "Remember how the LORD your God led you all the way in the wilderness these forty years, to humble and test you in order to know what was in your heart, whether or not you would keep his commands. He humbled you, causing you to hunger and then feeding you with manna, which neither you nor your ancestors had known, to teach you that man does not live on bread alone but on every word that comes from the mouth of the LORD" (verses 2–3). In verse 16, Moses says, "He [God] gave you manna to eat in the wilderness, something your ancestors had never known, to humble and test you so that in the end it might go well with you."

So the Lord led the Israelites into the wilderness (and kept them there for forty years) in order to humble them, to test them, and to teach them. Let's take a closer look at each reason.

To Humble

The experience in the wilderness was meant to humble Israel. The importance of this humbling is signaled by the fact that it is mentioned first of the three purposes, and twice in the verses quoted above.

To appreciate that emphasis, we need to know how the Lord feels about arrogance. In short, he "hates" it (Proverbs 8:13). That is strong language. But it is merited because mortal arrogance violates the first of the Ten Commandments. The prophet Samuel called out the arrogance of King Saul by likening it to the "evil of idolatry" (1 Samuel 15:23). Pride produced the first sin committed in the garden of Eden, and it plays a role in every sin committed since that moment. It is no wonder that the Lord was deeply concerned about this characteristic taking root in Israel, particularly when they entered the more comfortable living circumstances offered by the Promised Land.

So Moses offered these words of warning, also found in Deuteronomy 8: "When you have eaten and are satisfied, praise the LORD your God for the good land he has given you. Be careful that you do not forget the LORD your God, failing to observe his commands, his laws and his decrees that I am giving you this day. Otherwise, when you eat and are satisfied, when you build fine houses and settle down, and when your herds and flocks grow large and your silver and gold increase and all you have is multiplied, then *your heart will become proud* and you will forget the LORD your God, who brought you out of Egypt, out of the land of slavery" (verses 10–14, emphasis mine). Pride and arrogance have no place among God's people.

The Lord used the extended wilderness stay of Israel to humble the people. This transformation could not happen in Egypt, because it was a place that fostered arrogance. In Egypt, the Israelites were surrounded by a culture of human accomplishment, boasting outstanding achievements in language, literature, and technology. The highest things on the horizon were those designed and built by mortals.

In the wilderness, though, the highest things on the horizon were those designed and established by the Almighty. Wilderness is a place to take stock of oneself, a place where the looming mountains make us feel small, a place where humans feel the full weight of their own limitations. There are no grain fields, no flowing streams or life-giving lakes. Survival for an extended time is unthinkable without divine assistance.

In short, wilderness humbles. Here, Israel learned that the sum of who they were was not adequate to achieve what the Lord wanted them to do. Wilderness created the humility that formed the basis for the people's relationship with the Lord—and the foundation for accomplishing their mission.

To Test

Also mentioned twice in Deuteronomy 8:2–3, 16 is the second thing wilderness did for the Israelites: it provided the setting for a test. Tests are composed of questions that require us to make choices. The wilderness test question is not stated in so many words, but we can sense it when we stand where they stood. As Israel scanned the wilderness that lacks everything, the Lord delivered the arresting test question: Will you trust me here?

This question means something in the wilderness that it does not mean in other places. Consider how the question might have sounded in Egypt. There, the Nile River generates one of the most durable agricultural systems in the Middle East, bringing a continuous supply of water which is diverted via irrigation canals into the farm fields. During the annual flooding of the Nile, those farm fields received a fresh layer of fertile soil. All of this meant that those who lived in Egypt enjoyed a stable food supply. In Egypt, the fundamentals for survival were always in view. Will you trust the Lord in a place like this? Here where the need to trust seems less imperative, the answer comes with barely a thought: "Yes, Lord, I trust you."

But when you move the question out of Egypt and into the wilderness, things change. Here the question means more because more is at stake. There is no Nile River here. There are no farm fields. Now, the question of trust is personal and practical. In this place that lacks food and farm fields, God asks, "Will you trust me to supply what you cannot see?" The Lord used the wilderness setting to "test you in order to know what was in your heart, whether or not you would keep his commands" (verse 2).

This is a test. Will you trust me here, even when the fundamentals for survival are not in view?

To Teach

Third, the Lord used the wilderness to teach the people, when they were facing austerity, how capable, caring, and reliable he is.

God told Israel to turn away from Egypt and Canaan, places with food and water, and go to a place with neither. In this kind of environment, questions stir: Does the Lord know we are experiencing hunger pangs? Does he care that our children are dehydrating? If the Lord knows and cares, is he capable of providing for us as he promised? And if he is capable, can I rely on him to provide for my needs?

If we answer any of these questions negatively, we make the Lord into something less than he is. That is why the wilderness is such a powerful classroom, since the questions are met with positive answers. When the Israelites' hunger pangs surged, the Lord provided them with manna, a substance they had never seen before. In the absence of wheat and barley, this grain substitute was ground into flour so the Lord's people could make bread.

As they ate, the lesson was learned. God knew that the children were hungry. He cared about their hunger. In the wilderness, he could provide what no mortal could. And he reliably provided this special food week after week after week until Israel entered the Promised Land. In the end, the sure word of the Lord was better than any grainfield.

And, as it turns out, the empty wilderness was not so empty after all. It was actually full of lessons, particularly this one: "man does not live on bread alone but on every word that comes from the mouth of the LORD" (Deuteronomy 8:3). His promises were all that Israel had in the wilderness. But they were enough.

The wilderness developed the spiritual health of Israel in a way that Canaan or Egypt could not. The wilderness was not about punishment—it was the place where God could humble the people, test them, and teach them about his full sufficiency. The wilderness was helping Israel see themselves for who they were and see the Lord for who he was.

Why Does the Lord Allow Me to Enter Seasons of Wilderness?

If I could choose the circumstances of my life, I would pick an "Egypt" over a "wilderness" every time. In Egypt, I can purchase many of the things I need or want. In Egypt, I can enjoy my work and pay my bills. In Egypt, my family experiences good health and my relationships are happy and strong. I live so much of my life in Egypt that "easy" seems to be the normal, default position. It is how life should be. Then suddenly I find myself entering the wilderness. Like Israel, encountering the wilderness en route to the Promised Land seems like an unnecessary diversion. This is not the way things should be!

And my reaction is not always pretty. All too often, I lash out with language that is as embarrassing as that of ancient Israel: "Why did you bring the LORD's community into this wilderness, that we and our livestock should die here? Why did you bring us up out of Egypt to this terrible place? It has no grain or figs, grapevines or pomegranates. And there is no water to drink!" (Numbers 20:4–5). My focus is not on what I have but what is missing. I object to the disruption of the regular and pleasant rhythm of my life. I object to the loss of sleep. I object to the interference that fills my week with unpleasant tasks I had not expected. And the word I am most prone to shout is *why*. Why did you let me lose my job? Why am I struggling with this addiction? Why did you allow my daughter to die? Lord, why have you led me into this wilderness?

I don't want to oversimplify things, since the Lord certainly has many reasons for allowing my life to enter a season of wilderness. Each is unique and may have a special role to play in my life that we are not touching on here. But I cannot help but think that the explanation for Israel's long wilderness sojourn offers insights into how the Lord might use a wilderness experience in my life. Let's consider each of the three mentioned in Deuteronomy 8:2–3.

Could the Lord be using my season of wilderness to *humble* me? There are many things that can foster pride and arrogance during my time in "Egypt." Maybe I was told that I earned a promotion and raise because I was better than my coworkers. Maybe I work out regularly and eat well to earn the trim, youthful look others admire. Maybe I am just surrounded by technology and an array of scientific accomplishments that celebrate human effort and ingenuity. Oh, this is Egypt. And over time, this Egypt can foster just the kind of arrogance that the Lord thoroughly hates.

This vice distorts reality, giving me more credit than I deserve for what I do and who I am. At the same time, it also distorts my perception of the Lord and my relationship with him. To combat this, the Lord may allow my life to enter a season of wilderness to restore humility. When faced by problems and challenges that seem insurmountable, I feel my inadequacy. And it is not just the feeling of being overwhelmed—it is the reality of being in way over my head. It is knowing that I need more to survive a particular experience than I have inside me. Here I see my own limitations, and that humbles me.

Could the Lord be using my season of wilderness to *test* me? Here, we face the same question Israel faced in the wilderness, a place where the question really means something. The Father says to us, "Daughter will you trust me here?" "Son, will you trust me even when the fundamentals for surviving this experience appear out of reach?"

It is one thing to say that I trust the Lord when things are going well. It is one thing to sing about how much I trust him during a worship service. But the real test comes when we feel the press of the wilderness. God asks, Will you trust me when the doctor says you have cancer? Will you trust me when your spouse demands a divorce? Will you trust me when you learn your son is addicted to opioids? Will you trust me when you lose your house? Will you trust me on the day you lose your job? Will you trust me now? The way we answer means more in the wilderness. It is a test question designed to grow the faith that God has given us.

Could the Lord be using my season of wilderness to *teach* me? That is what he did with Israel, and their questions look very much like ours. Does the Lord know where I am? Does the Lord know what I am going through? Does the Lord care about the pain and fear I feel? Is he capable of helping when I need it most? Will he provide assistance on a continuing basis? Wilderness is the setting where the Lord clearly delivers answers to questions like these.

And the answer to each is yes. The Lord is absolutely dependable. Of course, all of these things are said many times throughout the Bible. Reading them is one thing, but *seeing* the Lord at work in our lives is another. As he provides, he teaches us just how trustworthy he is. And we learn how true it is that in the end it will go well for us (Deuteronomy 8:16).

——————————— Review and Reflection ———————————

1. When we enter a season of wilderness, how is Romans 8:28 helpful? How does it fall short?

2. What is the difference between confidence and arrogance? Why is one acceptable to the Lord and the other rejected?

3. What was the test question imposed on Israel by their extended stay in the wilderness?

4. What did the wilderness have to teach Israel?

5. What is your initial reaction when entering a season of wilderness?

6. How does the Lord's explanation for Israel's extended stay in the wilderness (Deuteronomy 8:2–3) help you manage your own season of wilderness?

5

WILDERNESS AND FAITH WITNESS

WHEN I ENTER THE WILDERNESS as hiker or climber, I need to pack a fair amount of gear. But along with that gear, I need to pack in a survival mind-set. There are no grocery stores where I can purchase food, no police force to provide protection, and no warm bed to welcome me at night. To make it safely through the experience, I need to focus on the basics, the things I need to survive: food, water, shelter, and warmth.

Wilderness seasons of life can also push us into a survival mind-set. When life gets hard, our focus narrows to what "we" need to hang on. We are easily consumed with self-care, self-preservation, self-attention. That means the question we are most prone to ask has to do with what the Lord is doing in our lives with these experiences. But there is another question we need to ask during a season in the wilderness: How is the Lord using my wilderness experience to benefit others?

You see, while we are busy "getting through" the wilderness, others are watching to see whether our faith wilts or thrives. It is one thing to show our trust in the Lord when life is going our way. It is quite another thing to trust God when life has taken a turn for the worse. So when we enter a more challenging time, others will measure the quality of our faith witness, a witness the Lord may be using to reshape others' perspective on life and draw them to himself.

This is the lesson the Lord teaches through a wilderness story from David's life.

A Wilderness Story

Before we focus on 1 Samuel 24, let's briefly consider what we have been through with David prior to that time. The Lord had sent the prophet Samuel to anoint David as king of Israel. The shepherd boy was destined to replace Saul, the first king of Israel, a man who had failed in his assignment.

The anointing in Bethlehem is recorded in 1 Samuel 16; the remaining fifteen chapters of the book invite us to do what the people of Israel were doing at the time—comparing the words and actions of Saul and David, the sitting king and his designated replacement. After David defeated Goliath and the Philistines in the Shephelah, the western foothills of Judah's mountains, Saul's resentment of David grew. Burning jealously propelled the king to make many attempts on David's life. In response, David chose to flee rather than fight.

That flight took him beyond the inhabited portions of the Promised Land, deep into the trackless wilderness. As Bible readers trying to trace David's movements in the wilderness, we find it as difficult to trace his travels as Saul did. That is, until we come to the start of chapter 24. Here the author of 1 Samuel clearly states in successive verses that David is in the Judean Wilderness at En Gedi (23:29; 24:1). This location was well known to the earliest readers of 1 Samuel because it was the site of a large oasis on the western shoreline of the Dead Sea, the starting point for a route that led through the wilderness into the heart of Judah's Hill Country.

What was it like there? At any given moment, the En Gedi region is both beautiful and hostile. Looking west, our eyes meet a series of high ridges and narrow gorges pouring out of the Judean Wilderness in the direction of the Dead Sea. The slopes are so steep and precipitous that it is difficult for humans or predators to walk them, making them the ideal place for the cliff-loving Nubian ibex. 1 Samuel actually refers to them when identifying David's hideout near the "Crags of the Wild Goats" (24:2).

The ibex, like human travelers in this region, need water. That is a real problem in the wilderness, where meager rainfall totals combine with steep slopes to carry away any hope of a lasting water supply. The eastern edge of the Judean Wilderness is classic biblical wilderness—without agriculture or permanent residence—until you come to the oasis at En Gedi.

Water is in the name of the place. "En" is a spring, while "Gedi" is a young goat. Thus En Gedi is a place where the wild goats gather to drink. The adults and their kids descend from the safety of the steep, desert ridges to drink water from the largest freshwater spring on the eastern side of the Judean Wilderness and graze on grass growing near the spring.

Where does this water come from? It had fallen as rain on the western side of Judah's hill country, where we would expect it to flow down the west side of the watershed toward the Mediterranean Sea. The surface runoff does just that. But the water that seeps into the soil is channeled *east*, under the surface watershed line, until it breaks out as springs on the Dead Sea side. It is this fresh, filtered water that pours from the En Gedi spring located on the ridges above the Dead Sea. Here the water tumbles through a maze of otherwise dry canyons, creating an unexpected burst of green that contrasts sharply with the browns and yellows of the Judean wilderness. The En Gedi oasis is alive with tropical plants, calling birds, and the rustling of wild animals. This wilderness oasis is the setting for our story.

A Survival Story

The wilderness setting for this part of David's story plays several important roles. First, it provides David with a place to hide and survive. David characterized this period of his life with this brief, compelling sentence: "As surely as the LORD lives and as you live, there is only a step between me and death" (1 Samuel 20:3).

These words reveal David's state of mind—he was playing defense, not offense. Rather than starting a civil war to dethrone Saul, David chose to retreat and hide from the king. He stowed away within the folds of the Judean wilderness, a location that gave him a real advantage over the pursuing Saul.

As a teenager, shepherding his family's livestock, David had spent considerable time in this ecosystem. By contrast, Saul's family lived in Benjamin, farming the high plateau. Israel's first king had had no need to visit the wilderness, and that difference in experience between Saul and David plays a role in this story. The complicated geography of the wilderness combined with Saul's inexperience there and made it possible for David to elude Saul again and again. Like the ibex, David used the winding canyons and steep slopes to evade Saul, stopping from time to time near oases like En Gedi to resupply with water.

A Faith Building Story

But the wilderness had even more to offer David. In the previous chapter, we saw how the Lord used wilderness to enhance the character and faith of his chosen people during the decades they spent there. The wilderness experience had not changed in the centuries that followed—and it accomplished the same things in David's life, humbling him, testing him, and teaching him trust.

The first words we hear David speak in 1 Samuel suggest he thought a little too much of himself. There is an edge of hubris to David's inquiry about what would be done for the man who took on Goliath, a tone to which his oldest brother took exception, calling him "conceited" (1 Samuel 17:28). It was just this kind of pride that damaged Saul's character and disqualified him as Israel's king (1 Samuel 15:23).

Read 1 Samuel 17 and then 1 Samuel 24. You will see that the precocious young man we initially meet disappears in the wilderness. David became more aware of his own limitations and more cautious with his words. The Lord used the wilderness to humble him.

Wilderness is also a place for testing and teaching. David faced the same compelling question that the Israelites did during their time in the wilderness. The Father asked, "David, will you trust me here, even when the fundamentals for survival are not in view?" David did not have a permanent home, agricultural fields, or a secure water system of his own. He was being hunted like a wild animal. And God basically said, "David, will you trust me now?"

He did. And as David trusted, the Lord kept teaching him that he was worthy of that trust. At no time during David's stay did he and those with him go wanting for the basics of life. In this wilderness setting, David learned the lesson his forebears had learned, "that man does not live on bread alone but on every word that comes from the mouth of the LORD" (Deuteronomy 8:3).

In the end, the wilderness was not merely a place for David to hide and survive—it was also a place for David to mature into the kind of leader the Lord wanted for his people, a leader after his own heart (1 Samuel 13:14).

A Faith Witness Story

David's time in the wilderness changed him. Just how much becomes clear when we read the account that begins in 1 Samuel 24. This wilderness survival story and faith building story is also a faith witness story.

The first four verses set the stage as both Saul and David are given unique opportunities. The only time that Saul catches up with the elusive David in the wilderness is when he gets some local help—Saul was told, "David is in the Desert of En Gedi" (verse 1). The king not only knew where David was, but he also had a superior fighting force. Saul had assembled a force of three thousand select soldiers (verse 2). David had about six hundred men, characterized as people who were "in distress or in debt or discontented" (1 Samuel 22:2; 23:13). Outnumbering David five to one in quantity, to say nothing of quality, Saul appeared to have the upper hand.

That is, until nature called. Saul went into a large cave that shepherds had used to secure their animals at night (1 Samuel 24:3). As he was seeking privacy, he unwittingly put himself in grave danger—the cave he'd entered was the very cave in which David and his ragtag group of fighters were hiding.

Here, the advantage switched from Saul to David. The king was without his army or even his personal bodyguards. He entered the cave to relieve himself without reservation or suspicion. The opportune moment for Saul had become the opportune moment for David.

That is how David's associates saw it, and they encouraged David to act. "This is the day the LORD spoke of when he said to you, 'I will give your enemy into your hands for you to deal with as you wish'" (verse 4). David's men were anxious to move on. They had spent months on the run with David. The early excitement of being with the future king of Israel on this adventure had certainly worn thin by now. And given the rigors of the wilderness, they were ready to end this life on the run and settle down in a more welcoming place. When Saul entered the cave alone, they saw their future changing—the path out of the wilderness and into a better life led right over the king's dead body.

David must have entertained similar thoughts. He and his men were trapped in a cave with thousands of well-trained soldiers just outside. Surely, a search of all the nearby caves was bound to commence soon. And while this one made a great hideout, it also left David and his men without an escape route when they were discovered. If they ran out now, they would be running to their deaths.

David knew that the Lord had rejected Saul. God had told Samuel to anoint David as Saul's successor. The moment of transition was coming and, by all accounts, appeared to have arrived. Knowing that Saul's death could solve so many problems, David crept closer and closer to the distracted king. But rather than striking Saul with his sword, David neatly trimmed a corner off his royal robe. Then David slunk back to the inner recesses of the dark cave, allowing Saul to walk out unaware and unharmed.

Did he lack the skill or courage to strike? Had he gotten squeamish? Hardly! This is the man who cut the head off Goliath. No, this was the restraint of a humble man of faith. At first, David's men did not see it this way. They were dumbfounded, even angry. But David prevented any of them from harming Saul by delivering sharp words that revealed just why he'd acted as he had: "The LORD forbid that I should do such a thing to my master, the LORD's anointed, or lay my hand on him for he is the anointed of the LORD" (1 Samuel 24:6).

David was also "the Lord's anointed," and he knew that one day he would be king. But equally important was what he did not know. The Lord had not informed David about *when* this transition was to occur or *how* Saul would be removed from office. David's men were anxious to fill in the gaps, and saw an opportunity that served David and their own interests well. But David filtered the opportunity through the lens of wilderness questions. He heard his Father's voice asking, "David, will you trust me now?"

In reply, David gave a powerful faith statement in both his actions and his words. Certainly, he wanted this stressful time to end. He was more than ready to end this life on the run in the wilderness. He probably felt the urgency of the Lord's call and wanted to get to the important business of leading Israel. But, more importantly, he wanted all of this to happen at the time and in the way the Lord wanted. Unless he had a clear word from God that justified the extreme act of killing the Lord's anointed, he would not assassinate Saul—no matter how easy or desirable that seemed.

When David exited the cave, the testimony continued. After waiting for Saul to walk a reasonable distance away, David stepped out, holding the scrap of the robe in his hand. He called to Saul, fell to his knees, and then splayed out with his face to the ground. This position of grave vulnerability left David defenseless. He was showing his humility and his respect for Saul—and demonstrating his trust in the Lord.

This posture made words unnecessary, but David went on to speak for what became seven verses in our Bible:

"Why do you listen when men say, 'David is bent on harming you'? This day you have seen with your own eyes how the LORD delivered you into my hands in the cave. Some urged me to kill you, but I spared you; I said, 'I will not lay my hand on my lord, because he is the LORD's anointed.' See, my father, look at this piece of your robe in my hand! I cut off the corner of your robe but did not kill you. See that there is nothing in my hand to indicate that I am guilty of wrongdoing or rebellion. I have not wronged you, but you are hunting me down to take my life. May the LORD judge between you and me. And may the LORD avenge the wrongs you have done to me, but my hand will not touch you. As the old saying goes, 'From evildoers come evil deeds,' so my hand will not touch you.

"Against whom has the king of Israel come out? Who are you pursuing? A dead dog? A flea? May the LORD be our judge and decide between us. May he consider my cause and uphold it; may he vindicate me by delivering me from your hand."

1 SAMUEL 24:9–15

Several things are worth noting here. First, Saul had largely operated like many of his ancient Near Eastern counterparts, kings who did not consider the Lord or his plan. By contrast, David repeatedly refers to the Lord's hand in all that has happened. Second, while Saul had referred to David disparagingly, David persistently identified Saul with honorary titles like "the Lord's anointed," "father," and "king of Israel." Third, while Saul basked in the royal titles, David—who also was the Lord's anointed—referred to himself in self-deprecating fashion, calling himself a "dead dog" and a "flea." And while Saul revealed his lack of faith by hunting down David in the wilderness, David highlighted the faith he exhibited in that wilderness cave by summarizing the near-death experience Saul had just faced.

In every act and in every word, David showed just how much his time in the wilderness had shaped him. He gave a powerful faith witness.

A Faith Witness Story That Changed Others

Those who heard and observed this interaction were changed. The soldiers with David in the cave had been highly motivated to remove Saul from the throne and install David in his place. They had urged David to act. If they had had their way, Saul would not have left the cave alive. But these men ultimately listened to David, respecting the faith witness he provided. After seeing it, there was no more talk of killing Saul. Now, these men too were willing to forgo the shortcut out of the wilderness. This was a change born of David's faith witness.

Yet the most striking change occurred in Saul. His early love for David, following the victory over Goliath and the Philistines (when Jonathan became "one in spirit with David," according to 1 Samuel 18:1), had changed quickly. The popular support that surged around David filled the king with a jealous anger that dominates the storyline until we reach the end of 1 Samuel. When Saul gave his daughter to David in marriage, he asked for gift that was sure to get David killed by the Philistines (see 18:25). Saul ordered his son Jonathan and his attendants to kill David (19:1). Saul tried to pin David to the wall with his spear in the royal palace (19:10). He sent men to David's home to kill him (19:11). Subsequently, Saul came very close to killing David at Keilah, Horesh, and in the Wilderness of Maon (23:7–8, 15, 25–26). On seven different occasions, in seven different locations, in six chapters of the Bible, Saul attempted to end David's life. If this man was going to change, something powerful had to happen.

It did. When David left that cave with a corner of Saul's robe in his hand, the king was overcome by emotion and regret. It did not take long for him to put all the details in place: he had been alone in the cave with David and his men. If David was close enough to cut off the corner of his robe, he was close enough to do mortal harm to Saul. The king's tears show the strong pulse of emotion, stress, and remorse he must have felt after being spared by the man he had repeatedly attempted to kill.

"'Is that your voice, David my son?'" Saul asked. "And he wept aloud. 'You are more righteous than I,' he said. 'You have treated me well, but I have treated you badly. You have just now told me about the good you did to me; the LORD delivered me into your hands, but you did not kill me. When a man finds his enemy, does he let him get away unharmed? May the LORD reward you well for the way you treated me today. I know that you will surely be king and that the kingdom of Israel will be established in your hands'" (1 Samuel 24:16–20).

This is the first time we hear Saul speaking in this way about David. Unfortunately, the change does not last—it will not be long before we again find Saul chasing David, trying to end his life. But if we pause the story here, we will see that David's faith witness was so powerful that, for a time, it completely changed the attitude and perspective of Saul.

Think about that: It is one thing for faith witness to change the attitude and perspective of a friend. It is quite another when that faith witness revolutionizes the character of a sworn enemy.

My Season in the Wilderness

As I work my way through my own season of wilderness, I need to be aware that the Lord may be using my faith witness to change someone who observes me. The Lord has given each of us "new birth into a living hope through the resurrection of Jesus Christ from the dead . . . an inheritance that can never perish, spoil or fade" (1 Peter 1:3–4). In turn, he asks that each of us allow others to see and to hear what that means in our lives.

Jesus said, "You are the light of the world. A town built on a hill cannot be hidden. Neither do people light a lamp and put it under a bowl. Instead they put it on its stand, and it gives light to everyone in the house. In the same way, let your light shine before others that they may see your good deeds and glorify your Father in heaven" (Matthew 5:14–16). The apostle Peter spoke to believers facing a significant threat to their lives when he said, "But in your hearts revere Christ as Lord. Always be prepared to give an answer to everyone who asks you to give the reason for the hope that you have" (1 Peter 3:15).

Those who do not know the Lord are always watching those who do. The unbelievers are particularly curious about how believers will respond when life takes a hard turn—when we as followers of Jesus enter a season of wilderness. It is one thing to let the light shine and give a hope-filled testimony when things are going well. It is quite another thing to do that when things are not. That is because such seasons stress our human resolve to the breaking point. Those who have experienced the permanent breakup of a relationship, or are met by a medical diagnosis that is terminal, or have faced personal economic collapse—among countless other hardships—are people in the wilderness. How will Bible-reading, church-going, Jesus-loving people respond when challenges like these invade their lives? Will their pious words become bitter and angry? Will their hope be replaced by cynicism? Will their lives pulse with despair and fear? Will they lash out at others and grasp wildly at any opportunity to leave the wilderness behind? Others will be watching.

So when we enter a season of wilderness, we need to think not only about ourselves but about the people who are observing us. We need to pray not only for the strength and resolve to get through the challenge, but to give a strong faith witness along the way. We need to pray for peace that presents to others as calmness. We need to pray for confidence so that we display hope. We need to pray that the Lord might be glorified by a light-filled testimony when the darker shadows of life fall on us.

This episode from David's life demonstrates that our time in a season of wilderness can deliver a powerful testimony that will change others. He sets a high standard, but one that I want to emulate. How about you?

——————————— Discussion and Reflection ———————————

1. Why does a season in the wilderness naturally turn our thinking inward rather than outward?

2. Why does our testimony gain power and meaning when it is given during a more difficult season of wilderness?

3. Compare the realities of the Judean Wilderness in general to those of the oasis at En Gedi.

4. What roles did the wilderness play in shaping David as the great king of Israel he would become?

5. Compare and contrast the perspective of David to that of his men when they saw Saul enter the cave in which they were hiding.

6. Characterize the dramatic change we see in Saul, and explain how the Lord worked to bring about this change.

6

WILDERNESS WITHOUT WANTING

"THE LORD IS MY SHEPHERD, I lack nothing." These words of Psalm 23, and those that follow, comprise one of the best-known and most-loved passages in the Bible. For thousands of years, Psalm 23 has soothed the suffering, comforted those facing death, and brought reassurance to people navigating uncertain times. Despite all this psalm has done, though, I am convinced that it can do even more when we put it into the correct geographical setting.

I would like you to try an experiment: take a moment away from your reading and enter "Psalm 23" in your favorite internet search engine to see what geographical settings are typically associated with it. I suspect your experience will be like mine. I found a flock of sheep grazing in a green field beside a lake with snowcapped mountains on the horizon; a lone sheep grazing in a sloping green pasture that stretched out of view; and a flock of sheep grazing beside a mountain stream flowing through a lush, green field. This is how Psalm 23 is most often pictured.

But that is not the setting in which Psalm 23 was born. This psalm is a wilderness psalm. And like all wilderness communication, it suffers when we extract it from that austere context. Taking this psalm back to its birthplace opens the path to new and powerful insights that are otherwise concealed from our view. That is why I make a point of reading and discussing Psalm 23 *in the wilderness* with every group I teach in Israel.

This is one of the most powerful moments of the study program I lead, because this physical context releases insights that have long been obscured by reading Psalm 23 against any backdrop other than wilderness. In this chapter, we will put this wilderness psalm back where it belongs—where it offers us this powerful reassurance: the Lord is our shepherd. And as long as the Shepherd is at our side, we can experience seasons of wilderness without wanting.

Psalm 23 Is a Wilderness Psalm

I would not blame you if you're reeling a bit from this chapter's opening paragraphs. I suspect that some of you may have even reread the psalm, thinking you had missed some obvious clues inside.

You have not. The term *wilderness* is nowhere to be found in these verses. In fact, the psalm does not contain a single shred of the wilderness vocabulary we find in other portions of Scripture. There is a good reason for that.

Psalm 23, like all the other psalms in the Bible, belongs in the category of poetry, and there are a few things we need to know and appreciate when we consider this genre of Bible communication. For one thing, Hebrew poetry seeks to say more with less. If something can be left unsaid, it will be. Specifics regarding the story that lies behind the poem or details directly referencing geographical context are typically absent. In this respect, Psalm 23 is true to form. We have no details of what was happening in the life of the poet, nor do we know where the poet was when this poem took shape.

So why am I putting this psalm in the category of wilderness communication? First, the content takes us to a pastoral setting, one in which sheep and goats were raised. The superscription of Psalm 23 (the brief statement that introduces the psalm) calls this "A psalm of David." David became the second king of Israel. But before he took on that role, he raised livestock in the Bethlehem area. And we know where the people of Bethlehem pastured their animals.

In the summer season, after residents had harvested grain from the farm fields near the village, shepherds brought their sheep and goats into those fields to rummage for kernels of grain left behind by the harvesters. As long as the grain was not growing in these fields, the animals were welcome, because they left something valuable behind—their manure enhanced the quality of the soil.

The picture changed in late fall and winter, though, when those fields were filled with sprouting and maturing grain plants. Now, the sheep and goats were not welcome. So the shepherds moved their livestock where grain could not be grown—to the edges of the Judean wilderness. There, the rain that matured the village grainfields also brought about changes to the wilderness. Dormant plants began to sprout in certain places, and isolated water sources began to recharge.

The people who first read this psalm knew that Judean livestock were kept in these two places—the farm fields near the village and the wilderness. And given these options, the language of the psalm best fits the setting in which the flock needed assurance that the austerity of the landscape would not leave them in want of the necessities of life. That setting is not the village farm fields but the wilderness pastures.

There is a second reason for reading Psalm 23 as a wilderness psalm: words and phrases within it echo language that appears elsewhere in the Bible to describe Israel's forty-year stay in the wilderness. The wilderness known to Israel was a place that lacked everything, and at the same time, lacked nothing. As Deuteronomy 2:7 says, "The LORD your God has blessed you in all the work of your hands. He has watched over your journey through this vast wilderness. These forty years the LORD your God has been with you, and you have *not lacked anything*" (emphasis mine). Or, as Nehemiah 9:21 puts it, "For forty years you sustained them in the wilderness; *they lacked nothing*, their clothes did not wear out nor did their feet become swollen" (emphasis mine).

The theme of Psalm 23 precisely matches the language I have put in italics: wilderness is a land without wanting. In addition, Psalm 23 uses a phrase variously translated as "valley of the shadow of death" or "darkest valley" (verse 4), and the prophet Jeremiah used the same term to describe the wilderness Israel experienced. It is the Lord who led Israel through a land of "drought and utter darkness" (Jeremiah 2:6).

Finally, the "table" filled with good things mentioned in Psalm 23:5 is referred to in the question raised in Psalm 78, a long song that recounts Israel's wilderness experience: "Can God really spread a table in the wilderness?" (verse 19).

As I mentioned earlier, poets seek to say more with less. That means biblical poetry will typically leave out a formal mention of geographical settings. But that does not mean the setting of a psalm is completely obscured. Given the locations in which the shepherds of Bethlehem pastured their animals, only the wilderness setting fits the language and message of Psalm 23. And given the words and phrases selected for the psalm, we are drawn again and again to that conclusion.

Reading Psalm 23 in the Wilderness

Now it is time to read the psalm in the wilderness. Verse one presents the theme that is echoed in the four parts that follow.

23:1	Wilderness without Wanting
23:2–3a	It Does Not Lack Provisions
23:3b–4	It Does Not Lack Protection
23:5	It Does Not Lack a Party
23:6	It Does Not Lack a Home-Going

Wilderness without Wanting (23:1)

The psalm begins by putting our focus on the Lord. Like the rest of the Bible, these beautiful verses are first and foremost a revelation of the one true God—and only secondarily about what that means for us. By starting this psalm with the Lord's name (and by using a special name for God), the poet puts our focus where it always belongs.

The name used for God is the one that he used when he connected himself to the covenant he made with Israel (Exodus 3:14–15). From the opening word, this poem is about that God, the God who is slow to anger and abounding in love, compassion, and forgiveness.

The inspired poet takes this wonderful name and links it to an image that was well known to the first hearers: "The LORD is my shepherd." This image appears throughout the Old Testament, and was used by Jesus himself (see Psalm 79:13, 80:1, 95:7; Isaiah 40:11; Ezekiel 34:12; Micah 5:4; John 10:11, 14). It worked well, because the people of Bible times knew a great deal more about shepherding than most of us today.

For those living in Bible times, sheep and goats met many needs. The sheep provided wool for clothing and the goats supplied the family with milk. They both provided meat for dinner and their skins became containers for liquids like water and milk. Consequently, most families had a flock of sheep and goats. These people lived the realities of the pastoral life, so they personally knew what it took to be a shepherd.

This was certainly true of David, the one to whom this psalm is attributed in its superscription. Before he became king of Israel, David was a shepherd (2 Samuel 7:8; Psalm 78.70–71). A man of the flock like David spent a great deal of his day outdoors, where he had the opportunity to reflect on many dimensions of life—including his relationship with the Lord. As he watched his livestock, it occurred to David that his relationship with the Lord was much like the relationship his flock had with him. As the Holy Spirit seized this moment, inspiring the thoughts and language of David, the words began to flow, creating the powerful message that Psalm 23 delivers. It is a psalm from *a* shepherd about *the* Shepherd.

What does it mean to have the Lord as your Shepherd? The answer is captured in these memorable words: "I lack nothing" (Psalm 23:1). That is saying a lot in any geographic setting, but it is particularly powerful when the backdrop is the void of the Judean Wilderness. We have characterized biblical wilderness as a land that lacks everything a human being needs to survive. David upends that idea in this extended metaphor, redefining wilderness as a place that has *all* we need.

It is not because David has forgotten where he is. He has recharacterized the space because his eyes have moved from the landscape to the one leading him. When the Lord is my shepherd, I can look at the harshest wilderness setting imaginable and say, "I have all that I need."

But what does that mean in practical terms? To find the answer, we need to remain at the side of the sheep and look at the realities of life through their eyes. When we do, we will find that the language of Psalm 23 probes four dimensions of the flock's life: provision, protection, a party, and a home-going. At every step, the inspired poet expands on the theme introduced in the first verse. When sheep look at the shepherd, they experience wilderness without wanting.

Wilderness Does Not Lack Provisions (23:2–3a)

The wilderness is an ecosystem where the need for provisions rises sharply even as the availability of resources diminishes.

Wilderness travel is difficult. While navigating the rugged terrain, the flock burns lots of calories. This physical exertion, in conjunction with warm temperatures, also makes it more difficult for the animals to remain hydrated. The shepherd must lead his flock to a water source and pastures multiple times each day.

But wilderness pastures do not look like the expansive green pastures on my grandparents' Wisconsin farm. Wilderness pastures are small patches of green scattered over dozens of miles, often hidden from view until you crest a ridge. Water resources are similarly hard to find and not near always the pastures. This psalm invites us to scan the view ahead, just like a member of the flock. When we do, the food and water so desperately needed are not in sight.

But the flock in Psalm 23 does not see what they lack, but rather what they have. "He makes me lie down in green pastures, he leads me beside quiet waters, he refreshes my soul" (verses 2–3a). The wanting wilderness becomes a place that lacks nothing whatsoever—because the shepherd makes it seem that way.

In the wilderness, there is insufficient rainfall to grow grain, so finding a previously planted grainfield for the flock is out of the question. Food is only available in the naturally occurring wilderness pastures, a product of winter rains that cause grass to sprout and grow. The shepherd knows that these flourishes of green will not persist throughout the entire wilderness, but some persist late into spring on the west side of rising terrain (areas that receive more rainfall) and on the northern side of rising terrain (where evaporation is reduced because north-facing slopes receive less direct contact with the sun's rays).

The green flourish that comes with the first rains dies back quickly. But the shepherd knows exactly where to lead his livestock to find the isolated places where life-giving greenery lasts longer. And in this case, size matters—the shepherd knows where to find pastures appropriate to the number of animals in the flock. The shepherd would not lead animals to an undersized pasture where the flock would be stressed by competing for the little grass that is there. Psalm 23 pictures an appropriately-sized pasture where the animals can eat their fill and then lie down.

The same is true of water. The rain that falls in the wilderness quickly rushes off the steep, impermeable slopes in the direction of the Dead Sea. There are no perennial rivers, lakes, or pools where a flock could be watered. But there are springs in the wilderness, fed by the rain that falls on the western slopes of Judah's mountains and then travels underground to the wilderness. Like the pastures, these are hard but necessary to find if the flock is to be sustained in the wilderness.

To be sure, the animals would obtain a portion of the water they need from the moist grasses they consume. But at least twice a day, the shepherd must lead the flock to one of these isolated wilderness springs. If the flock is to be "refreshed," it will take more than random wandering and the hope that pasture and water might be found over the next dry ridge—it requires the informed leadership of the shepherd, who brings his animals into regular contact with the required resources.

Following a shepherd like this makes the wilderness that lacks everything seem like a place that lacks nothing. Life goes on because "he refreshes my soul" (23:3a). The wilderness has become a place that does not lack provision.

Wilderness Does Not Lack Protection (23:3b–4)

There is no more dangerous place for the flock than the wilderness. To appreciate the shepherd's protection, we need to start by analyzing the risks associated with the wilderness.

Apart from the lack of food and water, there are travel concerns. There is a right way and a wrong way to move through this space. Wilderness terrain is steep, where a careless step can lead to a long drop and a quick stop. Such a fall virtually guaranteed a serious injury, one that would reduce the animal's mobility at best and end its life at worst (Ezekiel 34:4, 16). The right path to follow also took into consideration the places large predators liked to hide. Hungry lions, bears, and wolves kept a careful eye on the flock, watching for any member that was wandering, unwary, or injured (Genesis 31:39; 1 Samuel 17:34). Left to make their own choices, the flock might well dive down a path that offered the shortest and quickest transition to the next pasture or water source but, at the same time, put the sheep into harm's way.

So, once again, the shepherd intervenes. His or her reputation is, in part, built on route selection: "He guides me along the right paths for his name's sake" (Psalm 23:3b). When we see how many "wrong" paths there are in the wilderness, we can appreciate a leader who makes sure the flock travels down the "right" path—one that minimizes the risks imposed by hazardous terrain, that avoids places that favor large predators, and that keeps the flock together to diminish the chance for straying.

But what happens when members of the flock do begin to scatter (see Ezekiel 34:5–6)? The psalmist entertains that question in 23:4. The phrase "even though" could also be translated "even if." So the verse is saying, "Even if I walk through the darkest valley (or valley of the shadow of death) . . ." This risky place is not one where the shepherd would take his livestock. But sheep do wander, so some enterprising members of the flock will do their own route-finding. How will the shepherd respond?

The shepherd does not abandon animals that make a bad choice. Verse 4 says, "Even though I walk through the darkest valley, I will fear no evil, for you are with me; your rod and your staff, they comfort me." The shepherd does not merely call a wandering animal back to safety from a safe place. No, he dives headlong into the risky place, going after the wanderer and personally guiding the sheep to safety.

The words of the psalm present this from the perspective of the wayward animal. It sees the rod and staff of the shepherd. The rod is a club used to provide protection. The staff is used to guide. So even in a worst-case scenario, when the sheep takes a bad turn in the wilderness, the caring shepherd provides protection and redirection. This is the reality for the flock in Psalm 23.

Wilderness Does Not Lack a Party (23:5)

The language in the fifth verse takes a strange literary turn. Here we meet a new metaphor within the extended wilderness metaphor of this psalm.

The provision and protection the flock enjoys create an experience so different from any other experience that it must be expressed using a non-wilderness metaphor. In this verse, a sheep no longer sees itself in the austere and threatening wilderness but rather as the guest of honor at a human party.

Let's consider how far the reality is from the perception expressed by this verse. The wilderness setting creates anything but a party-like atmosphere for the flock. This is no place to play. There is no time to relax. This is a place where every ounce of energy and focus goes into getting through the experience. The laughter, fun, and zaniness of a party are completely at the other end of the spectrum.

And that is what makes this shift in language so arresting and powerful. Through the eyes of the flock, we are transported from the rigors and threats of the wilderness to a party scene: "You prepare a table before me in the presence of my enemies. You anoint my head with oil; my cup overflows" (verse 5). The threats (or "enemies") are still in this scene, but the focus is not on them or the terror, uncertainty, and worry they bring. The picture is one of overwhelming fun and celebration.

The shepherd-turned-host has provided the guest with fragrant oil to scent the scene. The host has set an opulent table filled with all the food one could want. The flock drinks without ever seeing the bottom of the cup, one that is refilled again and again until it overflows. This language transports us out of the wilderness to a scene that no sheep or goat has ever experienced. That is the point of changing the metaphor: we have not left the wilderness, but it seems like we have. Once again what is naturally lacking in the wilderness is not absent in this psalm.

Wilderness Does Not Lack a Home-Going (23:6)

This psalm that starts in the wilderness does not end in the wilderness. The final verse talks about the necessary and much-anticipated home-going.

For sheep and goats raised in a place like Bethlehem, the winter days that began in the wilderness would not end in the wilderness. There was good reason for going home: during the nighttime hours, the risk of being in the wilderness increased. It was easier to take the wrong path, to fall, to become separated from the flock, and to become prey of the predators who took advantage of the darkness. So as the sun dipped toward the western horizon, the shepherd led the flock back to the village.

Here the animals would be placed into a fold, a place where there was no risk of taking the wrong path or getting separated. Here solid walls stood between predator and prey. The day in the wilderness ended with this kind of home-going. And that is where the last verse of Psalm 23 takes us.

We can listen in on the flock reflecting on the day. It has been a good one, as the shepherd has provided and protected his animals: "Surely your goodness and love will follow me all the days of my life, and I will dwell in the house of the LORD forever" (verse 6).

From beginning to end, this psalm recharacterizes wilderness as a place without wanting. It does not lack provision, protection, a party, or a home-going. That is how the shepherd David saw his life in relationship to the Lord, his Shepherd. And when the Lord is your shepherd, not even the wilderness lacks what you need.

Seasons of Wilderness without Wanting

Psalm 23 belongs in the wilderness, but it also belongs in our lives. Given the way in which the lesson is presented, there are many different avenues with which to connect our lives to this psalm. Does your season of wilderness threaten your basic needs? Does your season of wilderness threaten your personal safety? Does your season of wilderness lack joy? Does your season of wilderness lack hope? The Lord is inviting you into the language of Psalm 23 to provide what is lacking in your life.

As you enter, realize that the Bible nowhere teaches that the believer's life is to be the life of a stoic. It never pictures Christians as people who need to just put their heads down and trudge the long and difficult road of life. We are not to be calendar keepers who just put an X through the date on the calendar, knowing that we have one less day to "get through it all." No—the Bible in general and Psalm 23 in particular invite us to see the season of wilderness in a way that others cannot: wilderness is a place without wanting.

But how in the world can I come to that perspective?

It is all about where we look. When we are going through difficult times, it is easy to focus on the horror before our eyes, the harsh reality of our wilderness experience. As a result, we find ourselves consumed by what we don't have. After all, wilderness is a place that lacks everything.

But here we are invited to change our focus. Instead of seeing only the austerity of the wilderness, we are invited to look at who is leading us—the Shepherd. This Shepherd stands ready to lead us to green pastures and quiet waters. This Shepherd will point out the path to take so we can avoid the worst of the harm that might befall us. And if we ignore that direction and strike off on our own dangerous path, he will not abandon us—he will follow us, protect us, and guide us back to the flock.

Our Shepherd can take a dark day and inject it with joy. We may not feel like going to a party, but we can at least get a bit of the party's joy. And in the end, we have this enduring word of comfort: whatever our experience, the time we begin in the wilderness will not end in the wilderness. At the end of the day, the Shepherd will take us home, far from the austerity and threats the wilderness holds.

We can be sure that our lives will enter seasons of wilderness, places that appear to lack everything we need. But in these moments of want, David invites us to look to the Lord. When we do, we can say with David, "The LORD is my shepherd, I lack nothing" (23:1).

————————— Discussion and Reflection —————————

1. Before you read this chapter, how had you pictured the setting for Psalm 23?

2. How can we claim that Psalm 23 is a piece of wilderness communication when the word *wilderness* is not used in it?

3. In the Hebrew of this psalm, the first word is "Lord." How is that choice important to the lesson the psalm teaches?

4. What comfort do you find in the words "even though" (or "even if") of verse four?

5. Why did the poet change the metaphor in verse five?

6. What is the picture in the final verse of this psalm? What does it mean to you?

7. How has the wilderness context of Psalm 23 changed your experience with this portion of God's Word?

7

WILDERNESS AND FORGIVENESS

THERE ARE MANY WILDERNESS STORIES in the Bible. There are many stories about forgiveness in the Bible. But there is one story that brings wilderness and forgiveness together in a powerful way.

It is the story of Jesus's first temptation. To be sure, all three temptations of Jesus provide a model for us, illustrating how we may meet and defeat the temptations the devil imposes on our lives. But let's be honest here: I need more than just someone *showing* me how to do that. Every single week I feel the frustration of knowing what I should do, but failing to do it. And when I fail, I feel guilty and fearful of divine punishment. I need more than a good example to follow.

What I need is someone to take my place, someone who can live the obedient life that I cannot. This someone is Jesus, whose mission included being my substitute. The Bible speaks about this substitution using declarative sentences, but in Jesus's first temptation, we *see* him living out that role. This is a story that demonstrates Jesus's willingness and ability to take on the devil and defeat him on our behalf. It is a wilderness story that speaks about our own forgiveness.

A Wilderness Story

The three gospel accounts of this story (Matthew 4:1; Mark 1:12; Luke 4:1) place it in the *erēmos*. This Greek word is used to describe a place without people, a place where wild animals rather than other humans provide companionship (Mark 1:13). It is not the exact equivalent of our word *wilderness*—Matthew uses it to describe the "remote setting" of the feeding of the five thousand, an event set near the shore of the Sea of Galilee, far from any true wilderness (Matthew 14:13, 15). But over half the time *erēmos* is used in the New Testament, it directs our attention to the austere wilderness—either the areas in which Israel spent forty years or the locale that provided the setting for the ministry of John the Baptist.

So in which *erēmos* did Jesus's first temptation occur? We begin to answer that question by looking at the event that immediately precedes Jesus's first temptation—the story of his baptism. John tells us that the baptism occurred at "Bethany on the other side of the Jordan" (1:28), just north of the Dead Sea. Luke adds that after Jesus left the Jordan River, he immediately went into the nearby *erēmos* to face his first temptation (4:1). This can be none other than Wilderness of Judea that lies just to the west of the baptism location.

Today Christians traveling the Holy Land are likely to visit Jabal al-Qarantal (Mountain of the Forty, a reference to the number of days Jesus fasted). This mountain, just west of Jericho, is where church tradition remembers the event. While it is in the Wilderness of Judea, Jabal al-Qarantal marks the spot of the event more precisely than the evidence allows. What we can say for sure is that the first temptation of Jesus occurred somewhere within this wilderness.

This setting is important to note because it introduces a high level of physical and mental stress into Jesus's story, making his temptation more difficult to defeat. Let's start our discussion with the physical challenge.

As I've mentioned before, travel in the wilderness is physically demanding, requiring lots of calories. But at just the moment you feel the need for food, the land you are traveling has little food to offer. For that reason, most wilderness travelers would bring plenty of food along—but Jesus did not. In fact, he does just the opposite of what we might expect: he fasted for nearly six weeks. Think about that. When Satan came to tempt Jesus, he did not confront a well-rested, well-fed man but one who had been physically weakened by a long-term lack of food.

The physically compromised Jesus was mentally compromised as well. Many of us have found that a limited time in the wilderness can relax and restore us, so long as we have access to food and water. But that is not the wilderness experience Jesus was having. He had been in the wilderness, without supplies, for more than a month. When people limit their food intake for this amount of time, cognitive processes are impaired. The ability to focus, to organize thoughts, and to reason are all diminished. Jesus's attention would have naturally and repeatedly moved between his need for food and his desire to get out of the wilderness.

We will fully appreciate this first temptation of Jesus only if we fully understand the physical and mental strain the wilderness imposed on him.

Temptation in the Wilderness

"Then Jesus was led by the Spirit into the wilderness to be tempted by the devil. After fasting forty days and forty nights, he was hungry" (Matthew 4:1–2).

These two verses set the stage for all that follows. The same Spirit of God who, in the form of a dove, had just descended onto Jesus at his baptism (3:16) immediately led him into the wilderness. Note that the Spirit was not leading Jesus *through* the wilderness, on the way to another location. The Spirit intentionally led him *into* the wilderness, where he would remain for weeks.

The Spirit then disappears from the story. But Jesus is not alone for long. Another spirit arrives, a less winsome being whom Matthew calls the devil. He is the fallen angel who led a rebellion against the Creator, the one whose sole passion is to ruin God's creation in any way he can. And what better way to do that than to attack the recently-identified Son of God, the long-expected Savior?

Jesus's baptism meant that everyone, including Satan, knew that this was the descendant of Adam and Eve sent to crush the devil's head (Genesis 3:15). Satan could hardly wait to attack Jesus, particularly since he was alone in the wilderness, weakened by a forty-day fast: "He ate nothing during those days, and at the end of them he was hungry" (Luke 4:2).

Matthew 4:3 tells us, "The tempter came to him and said, 'If you are the *Son of God*, tell these stones to become bread'" (emphasis mine). The words I have highlighted take us back to Jesus's baptism. The last thing we heard in that story was the Father's voice, booming from heaven, "This is my Son, whom I love; with him I am well pleased" (3:17). Now, Satan was urging Jesus to question the authenticity of that divine declaration.

The devil did not address Jesus as the Son of God. Rather, he said, "*If you are* the Son of God . . ." Satan's goal was to create doubt arising from Jesus's circumstances. How could the Father be pleased with his Son if he had allowed him to be alone and hungry in the wilderness?

I love taking my children into the wilderness. But I never would think of leaving them there, without food, water, and companionship. If I did that, what kind of a father would I be? That is the question the devil raised. How could Jesus honor and trust the Father who had left him alone and hungry in the wilderness?

So Satan presented himself as a concerned friend offering some helpful advice. When life gets tough, he intimated, it is better to trust yourself than your Father. The devil urged Jesus to perform a miracle that would both prove he was the Son of God and solve his hunger problem. The Father had done this for Israel in the wilderness. But he doesn't appear to be around now, Satan murmured. Jesus, it is time for you to act in your own best interests.

This mention of temptation, hunger, and food takes us back to the early chapters of Genesis and the Garden of Eden. Here, the devil assumed the form of a serpent, speaking to Adam and Eve about food and trust (Genesis 3:1–7). God had invited this couple to enjoy the food from every tree in the garden except for one. They would show their trust in God by honoring this directive.

But the devil tempted Adam and Eve to dismiss God's words and trust his own. The humans' unfortunate choice brought sin into the world, and the Bible records Satan's unbroken record of success over every human that followed. Even the great ones, people like Abraham, Sarah, Moses, and David sinned by failing to trust the Father. I suspect the devil thought Jesus might well crumble like each of them had. So, as he had with Adam and Eve, he used Jesus's hunger to initiate a temptation.

But Jesus handled this temptation in very different fashion. And with his words he demonstrated that he is, in fact, the Son of God. "It is written," Jesus said, "'Man shall not live on bread alone, but on every word that comes from the mouth of God'" (Matthew 4:4).

Note that Jesus did not reply to the devil's temptation with a new revelation from God. He certainly could have done so, but instead he quoted the Old Testament. And in doing so, he showed that the revelation we have in the Bible is enough to handle the devil's temptations. Notice too that Jesus used language from the wilderness to address this wilderness temptation. The words he quoted, from Deuteronomy 8:3, are part of a longer statement the Lord used to define the purpose of Israel's forty-year stay in the wilderness. It was a place in which the Lord humbled, tested, and taught. Here the focus is on the teaching: the wilderness instructs us that a promise from God is better than bread in the hand.

And that is what Jesus had—the Father's promise to care for him. Though he was ravaged by hunger pangs, Jesus's choice was to trust that his Father would provide what he needed.

Parallels with Israel in the Wilderness

Throughout this summary, you may have heard echoes from Israel's forty-year stay in the wilderness. This is no accident. Matthew tells this story from Jesus's life by selecting and including details that highlight the parallels between his experience and Israel's. Five things are worth noting.

First, both Israel and Jesus were led by God into this experience—neither Israel nor Jesus happened accidently into the wilderness. The Lord had led Israel by appearing either as a pillar of cloud or fire (Exodus 13:21). The rising of either one symbolized the time to move; the descending marked the time to make camp (Exodus 40:36–37). Though Moses walked in front of the tribes of Israel, he clearly states that it was the Lord who led the people (Deuteronomy 8:2) . . . and here is the very first thing we read in the brief story of Jesus's initial temptation: "Then Jesus was led by the Spirit into the wilderness" (Matthew 4:1). The same Spirit that had descended on Jesus in the form of the dove at his baptism led him on the next step in his journey.

The second parallel is geographical. The Spirit led Jesus *into the wilderness*—as we discussed above, this is the Wilderness of Judea. After Israel crossed the Red Sea, they also entered a wilderness, and Moses mentions a number of different areas that hosted the people: the Desert of Shur (Exodus 15:22), the Desert of Sin (Exodus 16:1) the Desert of Sinai (Exodus 19:1), the Desert of Paran (Numbers 12:16), and the Desert of Zin (Numbers 20:1). None of these is the same wilderness area as the one we enter with Jesus. But the same type of ecosystem—with all the challenges that wilderness has to offer—confronted both Israel and Jesus. Like his forebearers who crossed the sea during their departure from Egypt, Jesus moved from a water experience into a wilderness experience.

The third parallel is related to the number forty. "Remember how the LORD your God led you all the way in the wilderness these forty years," Deuteronomy 8:2 says. As Matthew tells this story, he notes that Jesus spent forty days in the wilderness (4:2).

Extreme hunger becomes the fourth point of connection. This ecosystem without grainfields did not naturally produce enough food to sustain hundreds of people for days, much less tens of thousands of people for forty years. To keep them alive, the Lord provided food—but it is important to note that the food did not arrive until after their hunger pangs surged. This is not due to divine neglect but a specific plan to transform Israel into the people the Lord wanted them to be: "He humbled you causing you to hunger" (Deuteronomy 8:3). For his part, Jesus fasted forty days and forty nights in the wilderness, allowing the same hunger pangs to surge within him. Matthew's simple statement builds the bridge between the two experiences: "He was hungry" (4:2).

This all leads to the fifth parallel, that moment when Israel and Jesus must answer God the Father's question. During Israel's wilderness stay, it is not stated in so many words—but it is implied in Moses's summary of the purpose of the experience: "He humbled you, causing you to hunger and then feeding you with manna, which neither you nor your ancestor had known, *to teach you that man does not live on bread alone but on every word that comes from the mouth of the* LORD" (Deuteronomy 8:3, emphasis mine). Food is important, but there is one thing even more vital than bread: the promises that come to us from the Lord. The wilderness experience of Israel became a daily test of their faith as the Father asked, "Will you trust me, even when the fundamentals for survival are not in view?" And Jesus faced the same question during his time in the wilderness. It came in the form of a temptation, as Satan said, "If you are the Son of God, tell these stones to become bread" (Matthew 4:3). Jesus and Israel faced the same question, a question that really means something when it is asked in the wilderness.

Substitution

Matthew wrote to ensure that we see the link between what Israel experienced in the wilderness and what Jesus experienced in the wilderness. By doing so, he illustrates that Jesus was willing and able to put himself in the same circumstances as Israel—but more than that, he was able to succeed where they failed.

"Will you trust me here," the Father asked, "where the fundamentals for survival are not in view?" Israel consistently answered, "No!" The biblical authors are not shy in making this point, and it is worth noting how clearly and often this is shown. From the very beginning of the wilderness stay, we hear them speaking like this: "If only we had died by the LORD's hand in Egypt! There we sat around pots of meat and ate all the food we wanted, but you have brought us out into this desert to starve this entire assembly to death" (Exodus 16:3). And at the close of the wilderness experience their tone had not changed. "If only we had died when our brothers fell dead before the LORD!" the people complained. "Why did you bring the LORD's community into this wilderness, that we and our livestock should die here? Why did you bring us up out of Egypt to this terrible place? It has no grain or figs, grapevines or pomegranates. And there is no water to drink!" (Numbers 20:3–5).

This failure was remembered centuries later in a psalm encouraging future generations to follow a different path than those who turned the Father's test of them into testing of the Father. "Today, if only you would hear his voice," the psalm writer urged, "'Do not harden your hearts as you did at Meribah, as you did that day at Massah in the wilderness, where your ancestors tested me; they tried me, though they had seen what I did. For forty years I was angry with that generation; I said, 'They are a people whose hearts go astray, and they have not known my ways'" (Psalm 95:7–10).

The memory of that wilderness failure persisted into the New Testament as well. "Who were they who heard and rebelled?" the author of Hebrews asked. "Were they not all those Moses led out of Egypt? And with whom was he angry for forty years? Was it not with those who sinned, whose bodies perished in the wilderness? And to whom did God swear that they would never enter his rest if not to those who disobeyed? So we see that they were not able to enter, because of their unbelief" (3:16–19). The wilderness experience was designed to humble, to test, and to teach Israel that a word from the Father was better than bread in hand. But the legacy of Israel's time in the wilderness is not one of success but failure—the failure to answer God's question well. *Will you trust me when the fundamentals for survival are not in view?*

This is where Jesus shows how different he is. He succeeded in exactly the ecosystem and under the circumstances where Israel failed. Jesus met the devil's invitation to turn stones into bread with language that defined the very purpose of the wilderness experience: "It is written: 'Man shall not live on bread alone, but on every word that comes from the mouth of God'" (Matthew 4:4).

Jesus's life and ministry would bring this out even more clearly. But even in the Old Testament, the idea of the Messiah as a saving substitute is mentioned in the words of the prophet Isaiah, who said, "He was pierced for our transgressions, he was crushed for our iniquities; the punishment that brought us peace was on him, and by his sounds we are healed" (Isaiah 53:5).

And substitution was assumed in Israel's worship system. In bringing sacrificial animals to the Temple, God's people were symbolizing this very principle. When Jesus died on the cross for their failures, he accepted the punishment for their sins in a way the animal could not (Hebrews 10:1–3). And on their behalf, Jesus would live a sin-free life, succeeding in exactly those places and in those circumstances where they had failed.

Our Seasons of Wilderness

The Lord and the devil view our wilderness seasons in very different ways. God sees them as times for us to grow in our faith and to demonstrate that faith to others. The devil sees them as times to tempt us to abandon our trust in God. So every time we enter the wilderness, it is no surprise that we feel the push and pull of this spiritual battle.

By their very nature, wilderness seasons take away things we need. Like Israel, that could be food. If the job you've enjoyed for years suddenly goes away, you may not have the money you need to purchase groceries. If you live in a large urban center and lack transportation, you may be caught in a "food desert" that prevents you from getting the provisions you need to feed your family. As you read this, you may literally be feeling the kind of hunger pangs felt by Israel in the wilderness. Will you trust the Father now?

Natural disasters can create these circumstances. As I write these words, the United States and its territories are experiencing hurricanes, tornadoes, and extreme flooding. Your home may lie in ruin. Your personal belongings and keepsakes could be swept away. Will you trust the Father now? Or perhaps your season of wilderness is linked to an aging family member experiencing memory loss. This is the companion with whom you have shared decades—and now your mother, your father, or your spouse does not even remember your name when you visit. Will you trust the Father now?

A season of wilderness makes us feel vulnerable, hungry, sad, abandoned, and discouraged. At these moments, the devil is more than happy to offer his own brand of advice, urging us to abandon our trust in the Lord. Satan asks, How can God love you if he allows this to happen to you? How can you wait on God's provision when he has not shown up yet? The devil's goal is to defeat trust and replace it with doubt.

I wish I could say that I've done well in these moments. I wish I could tell you that every wilderness experience has produced a powerful faith witness in me. But all too often, my voice in the wilderness sounds much more like Israel's. How about you? We raise our voices not to praise but to voice our anger. We don't declare our trust but forward our criticism. We demand to be taken back to "Egypt," that time in life when things seemed better and easier. The defiance feels good for a moment, but then it collapses into feelings of guilt. We have failed to answer the wilderness question well.

In managing my seasons of wilderness, the truth of the matter is that I need more than a good example to follow. I need someone to do the work for me—someone who can get it right.

If all Jesus does for me is *show* me how to handle the wilderness, then I am on the road to frustration. But peace comes when I recognize that Jesus came into this world to actually put himself into the life circumstances that I face. He did not opt out of the hard stuff. Jesus experienced the death of a friend, and the betrayal of a friend. He went through a civil trial that was anything but just. He did without food and a home. He put himself through every wilderness season I could experience—and in precisely those circumstances where I have failed to trust, he did. Jesus did this as my substitute, offering his righteousness in place of my sin.

This is a lesson on forgiveness that is taught often in the Bible. Sometimes it is relayed in declarative sentences like this: "For just as through the disobedience of the one man [Adam] the many were made sinners, so also through the obedience of the one man [Jesus] the many will be made righteous" (Romans 5:19). And the writer to the Hebrews uses the culture of substitution associated with Israel's priesthood to say it this way: "For we do not have a high priest who is unable to empathize with our weaknesses, but we have one who has been tempted in every way, just as we are—yet he did not sin" (4:15). This idea of Jesus doing what I have failed to do, offering his life in place of mine, is such an important teaching that it is said more than once and in more than one way in the Bible. And one of the ways it is said is in the wilderness.

There are many wilderness stories in the Bible. There are many stories about forgiveness. But there is one story that brings wilderness and forgiveness together in a powerful way, and we have just engaged it. I live forgiven because Jesus is my substitute.

——————————— Discussion and Reflection ———————————

1. How did the wilderness setting make it more difficult for Jesus to defeat the devil's temptation?

2. How does the temptation of Jesus link with his baptism? Why is that connection important to note?

3. How does the temptation of Jesus link to the story of Adam and Eve in the Garden of Eden? Why is that connection important?

4. Why did Jesus use Deuteronomy 8:3 to undermine the temptation of the devil?

5. Why does Matthew tell the story of Jesus's first temptation to carefully create a connection with Israel's experience in the wilderness?

6. How is this story helpful to you as you face a season of wilderness and its temptations?

8

WILDERNESS AND EXTRAVAGANT
LOVE FOR OUR NEIGHBOR

So far, we have considered wilderness stories that help us understand how the Lord uses "seasons of wilderness" in our own lives to mature and spread our faith, even as he shepherds us down those difficult paths. Our final wilderness story turns our attention to other people in a season of wilderness, challenging us to consider how we should respond.

These are people with whom we interact every day. They live in our homes or work beside us. We may share a property line or stand next to them in the checkout aisle at the grocery store. The Lord is as vitally concerned about their well-being as he is about our own. And when their lives enter a season of wilderness, he intends that we help them. That is why Jesus tells the wilderness story of the Good Samaritan.

I suspect you may already know something about this story. A certain man traveling the road between Jerusalem and Jericho was accosted by thugs who stripped him, robbed him, and beat him mercilessly. Three other individuals happened upon this unfortunate soul, each responding in a different fashion than we would expect. It is the last man, the Samaritan, who teaches the lesson Jesus wants us to carry away from the story.

Did you realize that this familiar parable is also a wilderness story? To be more precise, it is a wilderness travel story. The setting dramatically increases the peril the injured man faced, and highlights the sharply dissimilar ways that a priest, a Levite, and a Samaritan respond. In this chapter, we will see that Jesus used this story to ask and answer two important questions. First, who is my neighbor? And second, how extravagant should I be when showing love for my neighbor?

A Wilderness Travel Story

The story of the Good Samaritan is a wilderness travel story, though as with Psalm 23, the word *wilderness* is not found within its verses. So it is fair to ask what justifies our inclusion of the story in this book.

Jesus certifies its wilderness heritage by telling us that the action occurred on the road between Jerusalem and Jericho (Luke 10:30). Portions of this ancient trail survive, and I have walked a good share of it. So I can tell you from personal experience that for most of its seventeen-mile length, the road between Jerusalem and Jericho immerses travelers in the rugged and forbidding ecosystem of the Judean Wilderness.

To read the story of the Good Samaritan well, we need to become more acquainted with the realities of traveling this ancient road. A wilderness travel experience is unique from other travel experiences in the Promised Land, for three reasons.

First, the road between Jerusalem and Jericho is incredibly challenging, even by the standards of Bible-times travel. The elevation difference between Jerusalem and Jericho is thirty-three hundred feet. This means a steady descent toward Jericho and relentless climb up to Jerusalem. To be sure, the average change in elevation per mile is nothing out of the ordinary, but here is what the average does not tell you: the road between Jerusalem and Jericho climbs and descends repeatedly and aggressively as it fights its way through the rugged wilderness terrain. For every mile, travelers absorb hundreds of feet in elevation change that are quickly surrendered in a subsequent descent. This road is one of the most physically demanding and all-out exhausting in the land.

Second, the hike between Jerusalem and Jericho did not offer the opportunity for resupply. This road consumed calories at a stunning rate and forced the body's cooling system to work overtime. At the same time, it did not compensate by providing travelers with a ready supply of food or water. Those who used this road had to pack and carry the food and water they needed for the trip.

Third, the trip was dangerous. Supplies typically included a modest amount of first aid since the risk of injury increased here. There were terrain hazards, the risk of wild animal attack, and thieves who made it their place of business. If you ran into trouble, it was best not to count on the help or supplies of other people. Some roads in the Promised Land put you into regular contact with other travelers. This was not that road. If you had a problem, you were on your own. What you carried with you could literally spell the difference between life and death.

The people to whom Jesus first told this story knew this road. They knew that a trip between Jerusalem and Jericho was difficult and dangerous. It is not the kind of road you would use for a pleasant evening stroll. You traveled this road only when you had to, packed carefully for the trip, and lingered no longer than necessary.

A Single Question Leads to Others

The Good Samaritan story was told in the context of a conversation Jesus was having with a religious scholar. It was not unusual to find Jesus involved in a lively discussion, but his style of communication sounds a bit different here –because his discussion partner was not an ordinary, working-class citizen but, as Luke calls him, "an expert in the law" (10:25).

Within Judaism of the first century were scholars who carefully studied the Old Testament law code, defined in the first five books of the Bible. They loved to debate the relative importance of the details in those books and their implications for holy living. Jesus knew this man's backstory, so he engaged this "expert" with a style of communication that fit his place in society. As Luke reports,

On one occasion an expert in the law stood up to test Jesus. "Teacher," he asked, "what must I do to inherit eternal life?" "What is written in the Law?" he replied. "How do you read it?"

He answered, "'Love the Lord your God with all your heart and with all your soul and with all your strength and with all your mind'; and, 'Love your neighbor as yourself.'"

LUKE 10:25–27

The expert in the law raised a question for which he had already developed his own answer. So when Jesus turned the question back at him, he delivered an excellent answer, drawn from Leviticus 19:18 and Deuteronomy 6:5.

What Jesus says next sounds a little unusual: "'You have answered correctly,' Jesus replied. 'Do this and you will live'" (Luke 10:28). For the sake of the lesson, Jesus assumed the premise of the expert was correct—namely, that a person could achieve eternal life by living a righteous life on earth. By this technique, Jesus intended to highlight the man's failures and send him searching for a better answer than the law offered.

But the expert in the law pressed forward, assuming the law remained the answer to his initial question, even as he asked a follow-up: "He wanted to justify himself, so he asked Jesus, 'And who is my neighbor?'" (Luke 10:29).

Although the man's motives were inappropriate, the question itself is not. Both the Greek or Hebrew words for "neighbor" have a wide range of possible meanings. A neighbor could be anyone from a lovemaking partner, to a work associate, to a friend, to someone who lives nearby, to simply a fellow human being. The context of a conversation could narrow the scope of options, but the law quoted above does not offer either context or a definition of the term *neighbor*. So the question stands: Who is my neighbor?

Jesus answers the question by telling the story of the Good Samaritan.

The Story of the Good Samaritan in the Wilderness

The story begins when an unnamed man, presumably Jewish, leaves Jerusalem for trip that will take him to Jericho. Along the way, he is attacked by thieves. The details of the attack highlight its brutality.

The attackers stripped the man of his clothing, robbed him, beat him severely, and left him for dead. The wounded traveler was in desperate need of help in a place where help from a fellow traveler was unlikely. All things considered, it was unlikely that he would survive the night.

But fortune smiled on the crime victim. Not only did someone come along, it was a fellow Jewish man who, of all things, was a priest. Certainly, this man of God would know the language of Leviticus 19:18, directing God's people to "love your neighbor as yourself." Praise God, help has arrived!

But our relief quickly gives way to shock. The priest saw the injured man and then "passed by on the other side." To appreciate the callousness of this behavior, we need to realize that what we are calling a road is nothing more than a narrow hiking trail. The priest would have had to walk very near, if not step over, the wounded man! The religious man would certainly have seen just how badly injured his fellow traveler was. He would have heard the man's groans and plea for help. Yet the priest averted his eyes and scrunched over to the side of the trail so he could pass by on the other side (Luke 10:31).

But just as hope faded, fortune smiled again. Another traveler came into view—another Jewish religious man. As a Levite, this man belonged to the family line in Israel tasked with teaching the Torah to others. He certainly would know the language of Leviticus 19:18! For the moment, we'll assume that the priest who passed by was the exception to the rule. We'll expect this man of God to render aid.

The Levite also saw the man and heard his groans and plea for help—but mustered the callousness to do exactly what the priest had done moments earlier (Luke 10:32). Given the wilderness setting, what the priest and the Levite did amount to nothing less than a death sentence for the injured traveler. In the end, they appear to be as despicable as the thieves.

Then another traveler came into view—a Samaritan. This label tells us a lot about the man, and from the perspective of the injured man, this is not good news. The Samaritan story begins centuries earlier, when the Assyrians invaded the Northern Kingdom and exiled many of the Jews. The Samaritans are descendants of Gentile people the Assyrians imported into the Promised Land, "unchosen people" who intermarried with some of the Jewish folks who remained. Although their descendants lived in this land into the time of Jesus, they were fully Jewish neither in their ethnicity nor their theology. (You can read the story in 2 Kings 17:24–41; see particularly verses 40–41.)

During the time between the Old and New Testaments, a Jewish king from Jerusalem invaded the Samaritans' territory and destroyed the temple they'd built on Mount Gerizim. This event increased tensions between Jews and Samaritans, adding to the disdain they felt for one another (see John 4:9; 8:48). The Samaritans turned their ill feelings into action, physically harassing Jews who were traveling from Galilee to Judea. Luke mentions the Jewish/Samaritan tension just one chapter before the story we are studying (Luke 9:51–56). With these facts in our minds, we have little hope that this Samaritan man will be of more help than the two Jewish men who passed by on the other side.

But this Samaritan man is different. And the story goes on to describe in some detail just how different he was. By contrast to the first two men who ignored the wounded traveler, the Samaritan "saw" and "took pity on him" (Luke 10:33). He then engaged in a set of actions that show his love in action: "He went to him and bandaged his wounds, pouring on oil and wine. Then he put the man on his own donkey, brought him to an inn and took care of him. The next day he took out two denarii and gave them to the innkeeper. 'Look after him,' he said, 'and when I return, I will reimburse you for any extra expense you may have'" (10:34–35).

Who Is My Neighbor?

Once he had finished telling the story, Jesus turned to the expert in the law to solicit his take: "Which of these three do you think was a neighbor to the man who fell into the hands of robbers?" (Luke 10:36).

Within the story were a variety of responses to the Jewish traveler. Certainly, the robbers had treated him with heartless cruelty—they were not living out the good-neighbor principle. These ruthless individuals created the man's need for help, and the priest and Levite who happened across him should have stood in stark contrast. But they did not. In fact, the robbers, the priest, and the Levite all had this in common: they used the isolation and anonymity afforded by the wilderness to conceal their loveless actions.

Then there was the example offered by the good Samaritan. The cultural, social, and religious differences between the injured man and the Samaritan lead us to expect little from him, yet he delivered the most. "Which of these three do you think was a neighbor to the man who fell into the hands of robbers?" Jesus asked (Luke 10:36). It must have been hard for the expert in the law to admit it, but he answered, "The one who had mercy on him" (10:37).

The question of who is our neighbor appears twice in this story (10:29, 36)—and it is answered by the example of the kindly Samaritan. A neighbor is not just a family member, a person who lives in our village, or someone to whom we are connected ethnically or racially. A neighbor is a fellow human being in need.

The Samaritan, rather than the Jewish clergymen, got it right.

How Extravagantly Should I Love My Neighbor?

Jesus's story answers a second question, though one that is not formally raised in the story: How extravagantly should I love my neighbor?

For the answer, let's go back into the details of the story one more time. When we do, we will find five dimensions of the Samaritan's strikingly extravagant response.

First, he showed love despite anonymity. It can be easier to show love for another human being when we know that our efforts will be recognized. Yet here the Samaritan showed love in a place that virtually assured his actions would go unnoticed by all but the injured man. Remember that the road between Jerusalem and Jericho was lightly traveled. While the loveless behavior of the thieves, the priest, and the Levite would be concealed within the empty folds of the wilderness, the same setting virtually guaranteed the anonymity of the kindly actions of the Samaritan. His selflessness would go unobserved and his acts of kindness unrecognized, which makes his decision to stop and render aid so powerful.

Second, the Samaritan showed love despite risk. The wilderness is a dangerous place to travel, so the goal was to move through it as quickly as possible—to be out of this risky environment by nightfall. There was no room for unnecessary delay. When the kindly Samaritan stopped to help the injured man, he made a decision to lengthen his travel time in the wilderness and risked being on the road past sunset. The Samaritan would have been better off staying on schedule. But instead he showed love for an injured man.

Third, the Samaritan showed love by surrendering a portion of his supplies. To fully appreciate this, we need to remember that the wilderness does not offer the opportunity for resupply. Wise travelers carefully plan what to bring along for the daylong trip between Jerusalem and Jericho. Weight is always a consideration, so you don't want to bring too much food, water, and first aid . . . but you also dare not bring too little. That is what makes this detail in the story stand out: "He went to him and bandaged his wounds, pouring on oil and wine" (Luke 10:34). These first aid supplies (as well as the food and water he likely offered) were things the

Samaritan man carried to be sure that he could complete the trip safely. He did not surrender extras, but essential items he needed to complete his trip.

Fourth, the Samaritan showed love despite that fact that it cost him physical comfort. Judean Wilderness travel is demanding. You climb only to surrender the elevation you have gained in a descent before climbing again. And all of this occurs in the torrid heat of the desert sun. That is why the Samaritan man was using a donkey—it minimized the physical challenges associated with the trip. With this in mind, consider a detail Jesus includes in the story: "Then he put the man on his own donkey, brought him to an inn and took care of him" (10:34). The best evidence suggests that overnight lodging was available at either end of this road and in the middle of the route—the latter being the traditional Inn of the Good Samaritan. Getting to any of these locations meant more travel time, and now the Samaritan man would be walking rather than riding his animal. He surrendered the very tool that would have made this trip easier for himself.

Finally, the Samaritan showed love despite the cost in time and money. We are not told why he was traveling or what sort of schedule he had. But we know that he interrupted his trip to take time and care for the injured man at the inn. At this point, we may think the Samaritan had already done far more than expected. But that is when the financial conversation began: "The next day he took out two denarii and gave them to the innkeeper. 'Look after him,' he said, 'and when I return, I will reimburse you for any extra expense you may have'" (Luke 10:35). A denarius was the daily wage for a laborer in the first century. The Samaritan purchased care for the injured man with *two* denarii, then left the agreement with the innkeeper wide open, promising to pay whatever else was necessary in days ahead.

Any one dimension of the Samaritan's behavior is powerful on its own. But when we add them all together, we are overwhelmed with the selfless, extravagant love he showed to the injured man.

These details in the story of the Good Samaritan answer the unasked question, How should I love my neighbor?

The answer: extravagantly, like the Samaritan who showed love despite the anonymity, the risk, the surrender of supplies, the physical discomfort, and the financial cost.

Our Neighbors in a Wilderness Season

Our lives are destined to touch the lives of those enduring a season of wilderness. It is estimated that 20 percent of children, by the time they turn eighteen, will experience the death of someone close to them. Some one-third of the United States population will care for a chronically ill, disabled, or aging family member. Around 21.5 million people age twelve and older are challenged by a substance abuse issue. The list could go on and on.

Behind the settled façades of the people we encounter at school, at work, at church, and down the block, there lie troubling personal realities. The sheer number of those in need really challenges me. Where do I start? And when I start, how do I restrain the selfishness that limits the time, effort, and money I devote to assisting others who linger in a season of wilderness? Once again, let's consider the story.

The Samaritan was not assisting everyone, just the one person he met whom others could not (or would not) help. Here is how the apostle Paul explains our duty: "For we are God's handiwork, created in Christ Jesus to do good works, which God prepared in advance for us to do" (Ephesians 2:10). When we encounter that person the Lord has designated for us to help, he will make it clear that this is *our* neighbor in need. My task is not to help everyone—it is to determine where the Lord has prepared a service opportunity just for me.

The story goes on to defeat the tendency I may have to help only those who are most like me. All of us use social categories to define ourselves—and sometimes to define ourselves away from others. These categories include race, religion, ethnicity, gender, employment, wealth, politics, and education. We may feel most comfortable helping others who are most like us. If we narrow our definition of *neighbor* like this, we may well miss the person or persons the Lord has planned as the receiver of our charity. Jesus used the example of a Samaritan rendering love to an injured Jew to make sure that I don't excuse myself from helping people who are different from me.

Finally, this story shows us *how* to love our neighbor. Jesus calls for us to defeat the selfishness that might otherwise limit the assistance we offer. He wants us to show love extravagantly. This is difficult, because I am tempted to show just enough love to assuage guilt. But this story challenges me to ask how much—not how little—I can help.

So how much love is enough? For an answer, we could turn to many passages, but 1 John 3 is one of my favorites, working relentlessly to sync our idea of love with God's. The model is the love shown by Jesus for us: "This is how we know what love is: Jesus Christ laid down his life for us. And we ought to lay down our lives for our brothers and sisters. If anyone has material possessions and sees a brother or sister in need but has no pity on them, how can the love of God be in that person? Dear children, let us not love with words or speech but with actions and in truth" (verses 16–18).

These ideas about love are shown in action in the story of the Good Samaritan. He showed a love like Jesus has shown for us—an extravagant love.

The setting of this wilderness travel story and the actions of the kindly Samaritan join hands, challenging us to consider how we define and treat our neighbors. Now it is time for us to respond. Let's approach those we meet, people who are traveling through a season of wilderness, with the Samaritan's model in mind. As Jesus said to the expert in the law, "Go and do likewise" (Luke 10:37).

———————— Discussion and Reflection ————————

1. Give examples of times you have met people traveling through a season of wilderness.

2. We meet so many people in need of help. How has the Lord shown you where to put your love in action?

3. How does the wilderness setting of the story of the Good Samaritan influence the way you define who is your neighbor?

4. How does the wilderness setting of the Good Samaritan story influence your understanding of how to love your neighbor?

Appendix

THE BIBLE'S WILDERNESS VOCABULARY

Reference	Hebrew/Greek Vocabulary	Translation (NIV)
Genesis 14:6	*midbār*	Desert
Genesis 16:7	*midbār*	Desert
Genesis 21:14	*midbār*	Desert (of Beersheba)
Genesis 21:20	*midbār*	Desert
Genesis 21:21	*midbār*	Desert (of Paran)
Genesis 36:24	*midbār*	Desert
Genesis 37:22	*midbār*	Wilderness
Exodus 3:1	*midbār*	Wilderness
Exodus 3:18	*midbār*	Wilderness
Exodus 4:27	*midbār*	Wilderness
Exodus 5:1	*midbār*	Wilderness
Exodus 5:3	*midbār*	Wilderness
Exodus 7:16	*midbār*	Wilderness
Exodus 8:27	*midbār*	Wilderness
Exodus 8:28	*midbār*	Wilderness
Exodus 13:18	*midbār*	Desert (road)
Exodus 13:20	*midbār*	Desert
Exodus 14:3	*midbār*	Desert
Exodus 14:11	*midbār*	Desert
Exodus 14:12	*midbār*	Desert
Exodus 15:22	*midbār*	Desert (of Shur)
Exodus 15:22	*midbār*	Desert
Exodus 16:1	*midbār*	Desert (of Sin)
Exodus 16:2	*midbār*	Desert
Exodus 16:3	*midbār*	Desert

Reference	Hebrew/Greek Vocabulary	Translation (NIV)
Exodus 16:10	*midbār*	Desert
Exodus 16:14	*midbār*	Desert
Exodus 16:32	*midbār*	Wilderness
Exodus 17:1	*midbār*	Desert (of Sin)
Exodus 18:5	*midbār*	Wilderness
Exodus 19:1	*midbār*	Desert (of Sinai)
Exodus 19:2	*midbār*	Desert (of Sinai)
Exodus 19:2	*midbār*	Desert
Exodus 23:29	*šĕmāmāh*	Desolate (land)
Exodus 23:31	*midbār*	Desert
Leviticus 7:38	*midbār*	Desert (of Sinai)
Leviticus 16:10	*midbār*	Wilderness
Leviticus 16:21	*midbār*	Wilderness
Leviticus 16:22	*midbār*	Wilderness
Leviticus 16:22	*gāzēr*	Remote place
Leviticus 26:31	*ḥorbāh*	Ruins
Leviticus 26:33	*šĕmāmāh*	Waste (land)
Leviticus 26:33	*ḥorbāh*	Ruins
Numbers 1:1	*midbār*	Desert (of Sinai)
Numbers 1:19	*midbār*	Desert (of Sinai)
Numbers 3:4	*midbār*	Desert (of Sinai)
Numbers 3:14	*midbār*	Desert (of Sinai)
Numbers 9:1	*midbār*	Desert (of Sinai)
Numbers 9:5	*midbār*	Desert (of Sinai)
Numbers 10:12	*midbār*	Desert (of Sinai)
Numbers 10:12	*midbār*	Desert (of Paran)
Numbers 10:31	*midbār*	Wilderness
Numbers 12:16	*midbār*	Desert (of Paran)
Numbers 13:3	*midbār*	Desert (of Paran)
Numbers 13:21	*midbār*	Desert (of Zin)

Reference	Hebrew/Greek Vocabulary	Translation (NIV)
Numbers 13:26	midbār	Desert (of Paran)
Numbers 14:2	midbār	Wilderness
Numbers 14:16	midbār	Wilderness
Numbers 14:22	midbār	Wilderness
Numbers 14:25	midbār	Desert
Numbers 14:29	midbār	Wilderness
Numbers 14:32	midbār	Wilderness
Numbers 14:33	midbār	Wilderness
Numbers 14:35	midbār	Wilderness
Numbers 15:32	midbār	Wilderness
Numbers 16:13	midbār	Wilderness
Numbers 20:1	midbār	Desert (of Zin)
Numbers 20:4	midbār	Wilderness
Numbers 21:5	midbār	Wilderness
Numbers 21:11	midbār	Wilderness (before Moab)
Numbers 21:13	midbār	Wilderness
Numbers 21:18	midbār	Wilderness
Numbers 21:20	yĕšîmōn	Wasteland
Numbers 21:23	midbār	Wilderness
Numbers 22:1	ʿărābāh	Plains (of Moab)
Numbers 23:28	yĕšîmōn	Wasteland
Numbers 24:1	midbār	Wilderness
Numbers 26:3	ʿărābāh	Plains (of Moab)
Numbers 26:63	ʿărābāh	Plains (of Moab)
Numbers 26:64	midbār	Desert (of Sinai)
Numbers 26:65	midbār	Wilderness
Numbers 27:3	midbār	Wilderness
Numbers 27:14	midbār	Desert (of Zin) (2 times)
Numbers 31:12	ʿărābāh	Plains (of Moab)
Numbers 32:13	midbār	Wilderness

Reference	Hebrew/Greek Vocabulary	Translation (NIV)
Numbers 32:15	*midbār*	Wilderness
Numbers 33:6	*midbār*	Desert
Numbers 33:8	*midbār*	Desert, Desert (of Etham)
Numbers 33:11	*midbār*	Desert (of Sin)
Numbers 33:12	*midbār*	Desert (of Sin)
Numbers 33:15	*midbār*	Desert (of Sinai)
Numbers 33:16	*midbār*	Desert (of Sinai)
Numbers 33:36	*midbār*	Desert (of Zin)
Numbers 33:48	*'ărābāh*	Plains (of Moab)
Numbers 33:49	*'ărābāh*	Plains (of Moab)
Numbers 33:50	*'ărābāh*	Plains (of Moab)
Numbers 34:3	*midbār*	Desert (of Zin)
Numbers 35:1	*'ărābāh*	Plains (of Moab)
Numbers 36:13	*'ărābāh*	Plains (of Moab)
Deuteronomy 1:1	*midbār*	Wilderness (east of Jordan)
Deuteronomy 1:1	*'ărābāh*	Arabah
Deuteronomy 1:7	*'ărābāh*	Arabah
Deuteronomy 1:19	*midbār*	Wilderness
Deuteronomy 1:31	*midbār*	Wilderness
Deuteronomy 1:40	*midbār*	Desert
Deuteronomy 2:1	*midbār*	Desert
Deuteronomy 2:7	*midbār*	Wilderness
Deuteronomy 2:8	*'ărābāh*	Arabah (road)
Deuteronomy 2:8	*midbār*	Desert (road)
Deuteronomy 2:26	*midbār*	Desert (of Kedemoth)
Deuteronomy 3:17	*'ărābāh*	Arabah (Sea of)
Deuteronomy 4:43	*midbār*	Wilderness (plateau)
Deuteronomy 4:49	*'ărābāh*	Arabah
Deuteronomy 8:2	*midbār*	Wilderness
Deuteronomy 8:15	*midbār*	Wilderness

Reference	Hebrew/Greek Vocabulary	Translation (NIV)
Deuteronomy 8:16	*midbār*	Wilderness
Deuteronomy 9:7	*midbār*	Wilderness
Deuteronomy 9:28	*midbār*	Wilderness
Deuteronomy 11:5	*midbār*	Wilderness
Deuteronomy 11:24	*midbār*	Desert
Deuteronomy 11:30	*'ărābāh*	Arabah
Deuteronomy 29:5	*midbār*	Wilderness
Deuteronomy 32:10	*midbār*	Desert
Deuteronomy 32:10	*yĕšīmōn*	Waste
Deuteronomy 32:51	*midbār*	Desert (of Zin)
Deuteronomy 34:1	*'ărābāh*	Plains (of Moab)
Deuteronomy 34:8	*'ărābāh*	Plains (of Moab)
Joshua 1:4	*midbār*	Desert
Joshua 3:16	*'ărābāh*	Arabah (Sea of)
Joshua 4:13	*'ărābāh*	Plains (of Jericho)
Joshua 5:4	*midbār*	Wilderness
Joshua 5:5	*midbār*	Wilderness
Joshua 5:6	*midbār*	Wilderness
Joshua 5:10	*'ărābāh*	Plains (of Jericho)
Joshua 8:14	*'ărābāh*	Arabah
Joshua 8:15	*midbār*	Wilderness
Joshua 8:20	*midbār*	Wilderness
Joshua 8:24	*midbār*	Wilderness
Joshua 8:28	*šĕmāmāh*	Desolate place
Joshua 11:2	*'ărābāh*	Arabah
Joshua 11:16	*'ărābāh*	Arabah
Joshua 12:1	*'ărābāh*	Arabah
Joshua 12:3	*'ărābāh*	Arabah
Joshua 12:3	*'ărābāh*	Arabah (Sea of)
Joshua 12:8	*'ărābāh*	Arabah

Reference	Hebrew/Greek Vocabulary	Translation (NIV)
Joshua 12:8	*midbār*	Wilderness
Joshua 13:32	*'ărābāh*	Plains (of Moab)
Joshua 14:10	*midbār*	Wilderness
Joshua 15:1	*midbār*	Desert (of Zin)
Joshua 15:61	*midbār*	Wilderness
Joshua 16:1	*midbār*	Desert
Joshua 18:12	*midbār*	Wilderness
Joshua 18:18	*'ărābāh*	Arabah
Joshua 20:8	*midbār*	Wilderness
Joshua 24:7	*midbār*	Wilderness
Judges 1:16	*midbār*	Desert (of Judah)
Judges 8:7	*midbār*	Desert (thorns)
Judges 8:16	*midbār*	Desert (thorns)
Judges 11:16	*midbār*	Wilderness
Judges 11:18	*midbār*	Wilderness
Judges 11:22	*midbār*	Desert
Judges 20:42	*midbār*	Wilderness
Judges 20:45	*midbār*	Wilderness
Judges 20:47	*midbār*	Wilderness
1 Samuel 4:8	*midbār*	Wilderness
1 Samuel 13:18	*midbār*	Wilderness
1 Samuel 17:28	*midbār*	Wilderness
1 Samuel 23:14	*midbār*	Wilderness, Desert (of Ziph)
1 Samuel 23:15	*midbār*	Desert (of Ziph)
1 Samuel 23:19	*yĕšīmōn*	Jeshimon
1 Samuel 23:24	*midbār*	Desert (of Maon)
1 Samuel 23:24	*'ărābāh*	Arabah
1 Samuel 23:24	*yĕšīmōn*	Jeshimon
1 Samuel 23:25	*midbār*	Desert (of Maon) (2 times)
1 Samuel 24:1	*midbār*	Desert (of En Gedi)

Reference	Hebrew/Greek Vocabulary	Translation (NIV)
1 Samuel 25:1	*midbār*	Desert (of Paran)
1 Samuel 25:4	*midbār*	Wilderness
1 Samuel 25:14	*midbār*	Wilderness
1 Samuel 25:21	*midbār*	Wilderness
1 Samuel 26:1	*yĕšīmōn*	Jeshimon
1 Samuel 26:2	*midbār*	Desert (of Ziph)
1 Samuel 26:3	*midbār*	Wilderness
1 Samuel 26:3	*yĕšīmōn*	Jeshimon
2 Samuel 2:24	*midbār*	Wasteland (of Gibeon)
2 Samuel 2:29	*'ărābāh*	Arabah
2 Samuel 4:7	*'ărābāh*	Arabah (way of)
2 Samuel 15:23	*midbār*	Wilderness
2 Samuel 15:28	*midbār*	Wilderness
2 Samuel 16:2	*midbār*	Wilderness
2 Samuel 17:16	*midbār*	Wilderness
2 Samuel 17:29	*midbār*	Wilderness
1 Kings 2:34	*midbār*	Out in the country
1 Kings 9:18	*midbār*	Desert
1 Kings 19:4	*midbār*	Wilderness
1 Kings 19:15	*midbār*	Desert (of Damascus)
2 Kings 3:8	*midbār*	Desert of Edom
2 Kings 14:25	*'ărābāh*	Dead Sea (see NIV footnote: "the Sea of the Arabah")
2 Kings 25:4	*'ărābāh*	Arabah
2 Kings 25:5	*'ărābāh*	Plains (of Jericho)
1 Chronicles 5:9	*midbār*	Desert
1 Chronicles 6:78	*midbār*	Wilderness
1 Chronicles 12:8	*midbār*	Wilderness
1 Chronicles 21:29	*midbār*	Wilderness
2 Chronicles 1:3	*midbār*	Wilderness
2 Chronicles 8:4	*midbār*	Desert

Reference	Hebrew/Greek Vocabulary	Translation (NIV)
2 Chronicles 20:16	midbār	Desert (of Jeruel)
2 Chronicles 20:20	midbār	Desert (of Tekoa)
2 Chronicles 20:24	midbār	Desert
2 Chronicles 24:9	midbār	Wilderness
2 Chronicles 26:10	midbār	Wilderness
Ezra 9:9	ḥorbāh	Ruins
Nehemiah 9:19	midbār	Wilderness
Nehemiah 9:21	midbār	Wilderness
Job 1:19	midbār	Desert
Job 3:14	ḥorbāh	Ruins
Job 24:5	midbār	Desert
Job 24:5	'ărābāh	Wasteland
Job 24:19	ṣiyāh	Drought
Job 30:3	ṣiyāh	Parched land
Job 30:3	mĕšō 'āh	Wastelands
Job 38:27	mĕšō 'āh	Wasteland
Job 38:26	midbār	Desert
Job 39:6	'ărābāh	Wasteland
Psalm 9:6	ḥorbāh	Ruin
Psalm 29:8	midbār	Desert, Desert (of Kadesh)
Psalm 55:7	midbār	Desert
Psalm 63 (superscription)	midbār	Desert (of Judah)
Psalm 63:1	ṣiyāh	Dry land
Psalm 65:12	midbār	Wilderness
Psalm 68:7	yĕšīmōn	Wilderness
Psalm 75:6	midbār	Desert
Psalm 78:15	midbār	Wilderness
Psalm 78:17	ṣiyāh	Wilderness
Psalm 78:19	midbār	Wilderness
Psalm 78:40	midbār	Wilderness

Reference	Hebrew/Greek Vocabulary	Translation (NIV)
Psalm 78:40	yĕšīmōn	Wasteland
Psalm 78:52	midbār	Wilderness
Psalm 95:8	midbār	Wilderness
Psalm 102:6	midbār	Desert (owl)
Psalm 102:6	ḥorbāh	Ruins
Psalm 105:41	ṣiyāh	Desert
Psalm 106:9	midbār	Desert
Psalm 106:14	midbār	Desert
Psalm 106:14	yĕšīmōn	Wilderness
Psalm 106:26	midbār	Wilderness
Psalm 107:4	midbār	Desert
Psalm 107:4	yĕšīmōn	Wastelands
Psalm 107:33	midbār	Desert
Psalm 107:35	midbār	Desert
Psalm 107:35	ṣiyāh	Parched ground
Psalm 109:10	ḥorbāh	Ruined (homes)
Psalm 136:16	midbār	Wilderness
Proverbs 21:19	midbār	Desert
Song of Solomon 3:6	midbār	Wilderness
Song of Solomon 8:5	midbār	Wilderness
Isaiah 1:7	šĕmāmāh	Desolate
Isaiah 1:7	šĕmāmāh	Laid waste
Isaiah 6:11	šĕmāmāh	Desolation
Isaiah 14:17	midbār	Wilderness
Isaiah 16:1	midbār	Desert
Isaiah 16:8	midbār	Desert
Isaiah 17:9	šĕmāmāh	Desolation
Isaiah 21:1	midbār	Desert (by the Sea)
Isaiah 21:1	midbār	Desert
Isaiah 27:10	midbār	Wilderness

Reference	Hebrew/Greek Vocabulary	Translation (NIV)
Isaiah 32:15	midbār	Desert
Isaiah 32:16	midbār	Desert
Isaiah 33:9	'ărābāh	Arabah
Isaiah 35:1	midbār	Desert
Isaiah 35:1	ṣiyāh	Parched land
Isaiah 35:1	'ărābāh	Wilderness
Isaiah 35:6	midbār	Wilderness
Isaiah 35:6	'ărābāh	Desert
Isaiah 40:3	midbār	Wilderness
Isaiah 40:3	'ărābāh	Desert
Isaiah 41:18	midbār	Desert
Isaiah 41:18	ṣiyāh	Parched ground
Isaiah 41:19	midbār	Desert
Isaiah 41:19	'ărābāh	Wasteland
Isaiah 42:11	midbār	Wilderness
Isaiah 43:19	midbār	Wilderness
Isaiah 43:19	yĕšīmōn	Wasteland
Isaiah 43:20	midbār	Wilderness
Isaiah 43:20	yĕšīmōn	Wasteland
Isaiah 48:21	ḥorbāh	Deserts
Isaiah 49:19	ḥorbāh	Ruined
Isaiah 50:2	midbār	Desert
Isaiah 51:3	ḥorbāh	Ruins
Isaiah 51:3	midbār	Deserts
Isaiah 51:3	'ărābāh	Wastelands
Isaiah 52:9	ḥorbāh	Ruins
Isaiah 53:2	ṣiyāh	Dry ground
Isaiah 58:11	ṣaḥṣāḥāh	Sun-scorched (land)
Isaiah 58:12	ḥorbāh	Ruins
Isaiah 61:4	ḥorbāh	Ruins

Reference	Hebrew/Greek Vocabulary	Translation (NIV)
Isaiah 62:4	*šĕmāmāh*	Desolate
Isaiah 63:13	*midbār*	Open country
Isaiah 64:10	*midbār*	Wasteland (2 times)
Isaiah 64:10	*šĕmāmāh*	Desolation
Isaiah 64:11	*ḥorbāh*	Ruins
Jeremiah 2:2	*midbār*	Wilderness
Jeremiah 2:6	*midbār*	Wilderness
Jeremiah 2:6	*'ărābāh*	Deserts
Jeremiah 2:6	*ṣiyāh*	Land of drought
Jeremiah 2:24	*midbār*	Desert
Jeremiah 2:31	*midbār*	Desert
Jeremiah 3:2	*midbār*	Desert
Jeremiah 4:11	*midbār*	Desert
Jeremiah 4:26	*midbār*	Desert
Jeremiah 4:27	*šĕmāmāh*	Ruined (land)
Jeremiah 5:6	*'ărābāh*	Desert
Jeremiah 6:8	*šĕmāmāh*	Desolate (land)
Jeremiah 7:34	*ḥorbāh*	Desolate
Jeremiah 9:2	*midbār*	Desert
Jeremiah 9:10	*midbār*	Wilderness
Jeremiah 9:11	*šĕmāmāh*	Laid waste
Jeremiah 9:12	*midbār*	Desert
Jeremiah 9:26	*midbār*	Wilderness
Jeremiah 10:22	*šĕmāmāh*	Desolate
Jeremiah 12:10	*šĕmāmāh*	Desolate
Jeremiah 12:10	*midbār*	Wasteland
Jeremiah 12:11	*šĕmāmāh*	Wasteland
Jeremiah 12:12	*midbār*	Desert
Jeremiah 13:24	*midbār*	Desert (wind)
Jeremiah 17:6	*'ărābāh*	Wastelands

Reference	Hebrew/Greek Vocabulary	Translation (NIV)
Jeremiah 17:6	midbār	Desert
Jeremiah 22:5	ḥorbāh	Ruin
Jeremiah 22:6	midbār	Wasteland
Jeremiah 23:10	midbār	Wilderness
Jeremiah 25:9	ḥorbāh	Ruin
Jeremiah 25:11	ḥorbāh	Desolate
Jeremiah 25:12	šĕmāmāh	Desolate
Jeremiah 25:18	ḥorbāh	Ruin
Jeremiah 25:24	midbār	Wilderness
Jeremiah 27:17	ḥorbāh	Ruin
Jeremiah 31:2	midbār	Wilderness
Jeremiah 32:43	šĕmāmāh	Desolate waste
Jeremiah 34:22	šĕmāmāh	Lay waste
Jeremiah 39:4	ʿărābāh	Arabah
Jeremiah 39:5	ʿărābāh	Plains (of Jericho)
Jeremiah 44:2	ḥorbāh	Ruins
Jeremiah 44:6	šĕmāmāh	Desolate
Jeremiah 44:6	ḥorbāh	Ruins
Jeremiah 44:22	ḥorbāh	Desolate
Jeremiah 48:6	midbār	Desert
Jeremiah 49:2	šĕmāmāh	Ruins
Jeremiah 49:13	ḥorbāh	Ruin
Jeremiah 49:33	šĕmāmāh	Desolate Place
Jeremiah 50:12	midbār	Wilderness
Jeremiah 50:12	ṣiyāh	Dry land
Jeremiah 50:12	ʿărābāh	Desert
Jeremiah 50:13	šĕmāmāh	Desolate
Jeremiah 51:26	šĕmāmāh	Desolate
Jeremiah 51:43	ṣiyāh	Dry land
Jeremiah 51:43	ʿărābāh	Desert (land)

Reference	Hebrew/Greek Vocabulary	Translation (NIV)
Jeremiah 51:62	šĕmāmāh	Desolate
Jeremiah 52:7	'ărābāh	Arabah
Jeremiah 52:8	'ărābāh	Plains (of Jericho)
Lamentations 4:3	midbār	Desert
Lamentations 4:19	midbār	Desert
Lamentations 5:9	midbār	Desert
Ezekiel 5:14	ḥorbāh	Ruin
Ezekiel 6:14	šĕmāmāh	Desolate waste
Ezekiel 6:14	midbār	Desert
Ezekiel 7:27	šĕmāmāh	Despair
Ezekiel 12:20	šĕmāmāh	Desolate (land)
Ezekiel 13:4	ḥorbāh	Ruins
Ezekiel 14:15	šĕmāmāh	Desolate
Ezekiel 15:8	šĕmāmāh	Desolate (land)
Ezekiel 19:13	midbār	Desert
Ezekiel 19:13	ṣiyāh	Dry (land)
Ezekiel 20:10	midbār	Wilderness
Ezekiel 20:13	midbār	Wilderness (2 times)
Ezekiel 20:15	midbār	Wilderness
Ezekiel 20:17	midbār	Wilderness
Ezekiel 20:18	midbār	Wilderness
Ezekiel 20:21	midbār	Wilderness
Ezekiel 20:23	midbār	Wilderness
Ezekiel 20:35	midbār	Wilderness
Ezekiel 20:36	midbār	Wilderness
Ezekiel 23:33	šĕmāmāh	Desolation
Ezekiel 23:42	midbār	Desert
Ezekiel 25:13	ḥorbāh	Waste
Ezekiel 26:20	ḥorbāh	Ruins
Ezekiel 29:5	midbār	Desert

Reference	Hebrew/Greek Vocabulary	Translation (NIV)
Ezekiel 29:9	šĕmāmāh	Desolate
Ezekiel 29:9	ḥorbāh	Wasteland
Ezekiel 29:10	šĕmāmāh	Desolate waste
Ezekiel 29:12	šĕmāmāh	Desolate (2 times)
Ezekiel 32:15	šĕmāmāh	Desolate
Ezekiel 33:24	ḥorbāh	Ruins
Ezekiel 33:27	ḥorbāh	Ruins
Ezekiel 33:28	šĕmāmāh	Desolate waste
Ezekiel 33:29	šĕmāmāh	Desolate waste
Ezekiel 35:3	šĕmāmāh	Desolate waste
Ezekiel 35:4	ḥorbāh	Ruins
Ezekiel 35:4	šĕmāmāh	Desolate
Ezekiel 35:7	šĕmāmāh	Desolate waste
Ezekiel 35:9	šĕmāmāh	Desolate
Ezekiel 35:14	šĕmāmāh	Desolate
Ezekiel 35:15	šĕmāmāh	Desolate
Ezekiel 34:25	midbār	Wilderness
Ezekiel 36:4	šĕmāmāh	Desolate
Ezekiel 36:4	ḥorbāh	Ruins
Ezekiel 36:10	ḥorbāh	Ruins
Ezekiel 36:33	ḥorbāh	Ruins
Ezekiel 36:34	šĕmāmāh	Desolate
Ezekiel 38:8	ḥorbāh	Desolate
Ezekiel 38:12	ḥorbāh	Ruins
Ezekiel 47:8	ʿărābāh	Arabah
Hosea 2:3	midbār	Desert
Hosea 2:3	ṣiyāh	Parched land
Hosea 2:14	midbār	Wilderness
Hosea 9:10	midbār	Desert
Hosea 13:5	midbār	Wilderness

Reference	Hebrew/Greek Vocabulary	Translation (NIV)
Hosea 13:15	midbār	Desert
Joel 1:19	midbār	Wilderness
Joel 1:20	midbār	Wilderness
Joel 2:3	midbār	Desert
Joel 2:3	šĕmāmāh	Waste
Joel 2:20	ṣiyāh	Parched (land)
Joel 2:20	šĕmāmāh	Barren land
Joel 2:22	midbār	Wilderness
Joel 3:19	šĕmāmāh	Desolate
Joel 3:19	midbār	Desert waste
Amos 2:10	midbār	Wilderness
Amos 5:25	midbār	Wilderness
Amos 6:14	ʿărābāh	Arabah
Micah 1:7	šĕmāmāh	Broken in pieces
Micah 7:13	šĕmāmāh	Desolate
Zephaniah 1:13	šĕmāmāh	Demolished (homes)
Zephaniah 1:15	mĕšōʾāh	Ruin
Zephaniah 2:4	šĕmāmāh	Left in ruins
Zephaniah 2:9	šĕmāmāh	Wasteland
Zephaniah 2:13	šĕmāmāh	Utterly desolate
Zephaniah 2:13	ṣiyāh	Dry
Zephaniah 2:13	midbār	Desert
Zechariah 14:10	ʿărābāh	Arabah
Malachi 1:3	šĕmāmāh	Wasteland
Malachi 1:3	midbār	Desert (jackals)
Malachi 1:4	ḥorbāh	Ruins
Matthew 3:1	erēmos	Wilderness (of Judea)
Matthew 3:3	erēmos	Wilderness
Matthew 4:1	erēmos	Wilderness
Matthew 11:7	erēmos	Wilderness

Reference	Hebrew/Greek Vocabulary	Translation (NIV)
Matthew 23:38	*erēmos*	Desolate
Matthew 24:26	*erēmos*	Wilderness
Mark 1:3	*erēmos*	Wilderness
Mark 1:4	*erēmos*	Wilderness
Mark 1:12	*erēmos*	Wilderness
Mark 1:13	*erēmos*	Wilderness
Luke 1:80	*erēmos*	Wilderness
Luke 3:2	*erēmos*	Wilderness
Luke 3:4	*erēmos*	Wilderness
Luke 4:1	*erēmos*	Wilderness
Luke 7:24	*erēmos*	Wilderness
Luke 15:4	*erēmos*	Open country
John 1:23	*erēmos*	Wilderness
John 3:14	*erēmos*	Wilderness
John 6:31	*erēmos*	Wilderness
John 6:49	*erēmos*	Wilderness
John 11:54	*erēmos*	Wilderness
Acts 1:20	*erēmos*	Deserted (place)
Acts 7:30	*erēmos*	Desert
Acts 7:36	*erēmos*	Wilderness
Acts 7:38	*erēmos*	Wilderness
Acts 7:42	*erēmos*	Wilderness
Acts 7:44	*erēmos*	Wilderness
Acts 8:26	*erēmos*	Desert (road)
Acts 13:18	*erēmos*	Wilderness
Acts 21:38	*erēmos*	Wilderness
1 Corinthians 10:5	*erēmos*	Wilderness
Hebrews 3:8	*erēmos*	Wilderness
Hebrews 3:17	*erēmos*	Wilderness
Hebrews 11:38	*erimia*	Deserts

Reference	Hebrew/Greek Vocabulary	Translation (NIV)
Revelation 12:6	*erēmos*	Wilderness
Revelation 12:14	*erēmos*	Wilderness
Revelation 17:3	*erēmos*	Wilderness

NOTES

Introduction

1. John Muir, *Steep Trails* (Boston: Houghton Mifflin Company, 1918), 128.
2. John Muir, *Our National Parks* (Boston: Houghton Mifflin, 1901), 56.
3. Aldo Leopold, *A Sand County Almanac* (New York: Ballantine Books, 1970), xviii–xix.
4. Roderick Frazier Nash, *Wilderness and the American Mind* (New Haven, Connecticut: Yale University Press, 2001), 36–37.
5. Ibid., 41.
6. Ibid., 84.
7. Ibid., 125.

Chapter 2: Why Wilderness?

1. Ibid, 8.

Chapter 3: What Is Wilderness?

1. Aldo Leopold, "The Wilderness and Its Place in Forest Recreational Policy," *Journal of Forestry* 19 (1921): 18–21.
2. *Wilderness Act*, Public Law 88-577, 16 U.S. C. 1131-1136 (1964), Section 2, c.
3. For more on this subject, see John A. Beck, *Zondervan Dictionary of Biblical Imagery* (Grand Rapids, Michigan: Zondervan, 2011), 110–12.

4. George Adam Smith, *The Historical Geography of the Holy Land, Especially in Relation to the History of Israel and of the Early Church* (London: Hodder and Stoughton, 1897), 316.

5. Ibid., 314.

6. Linnie Marsh Wolfe, ed., *John of the Mountains: The Unpublished Journals of John Muir* (Madison, Wisconsin: University of Wisconsin Press, 1938), 439.

Land without Borders
VIDEO STUDY GUIDE

The following material is based on author John Beck's six-part video study entitled *Land without Borders*. Filmed on location in the wilderness areas of Israel, the videos give us a fascinating introduction to the rough, austere hills and valleys of biblical wilderness locations. Although the book and the videos stand alone, they may be combined for the greatest study benefit. Each video episode outline will direct you to the related chapter in this book.

Episode 1: What Is Wilderness?

Episode 2: How Does God Use Wilderness?

Episode 3: Wilderness and Faith Witness

Episode 4: Wilderness without Wanting

Episode 5: Wilderness and Forgiveness

Episode 6: Wilderness and Extravagant Love for Our Neighbor

——————————————— Episode 1 ———————————————

WHAT IS WILDERNESS?

Additional Reading: *Land without Borders* chapter 3, "What Is Wilderness?"

Scripture Connection: Jeremiah 2:6

PROLOGUE

According to Dr. John Beck, there are more than 300 biblical references to the ecosystem we recognize as wilderness. But what is the significance of this term as Bible authors used it? Dr. Beck treks into the wilderness to help us understand seven specific characteristics of the wilderness up close, and this will help us grasp what the writers were talking about when they spoke of this often barren landscape.

LOOKING BACK ON THE JOURNEY

Questions for consideration and discussion

1. Dr. Beck suggests that as he explains the biblical wilderness, we might have to change our thinking about what a wilderness is. What does he mean by that statement? What is he assuming we might already know about wilderness?

2. The first similarity shared by all biblical wilderness areas is that it they are _____ and _____. Dr. Beck explains that the wilderness where he and his students are standing is just

twelve miles from Jerusalem, and then he gives its dimensions. What surprises you as he explains these things?

3. Dr. Beck goes on to give the second characteristic of a biblical wilderness: It has precious little _____. What keeps the rains from the Mediterranean Sea from reaching these arid pieces of land?

4. The group moves on to other landscapes, the Wilderness of Paran and the Wilderness of Zin. Here Dr. Beck continues to explain the shared traits of the wilderness. The third trait is that it has very little grain. How does that trait differ from the second trait? And what is the major problem this causes for anyone trying to live in a wilderness?

5. The fourth characteristic is that wilderness is a land of limited permanent _____. One of the main reasons for this is connected to the third trait. Explain how trait three leads to trait four.

6. It is logical then, that this vast, rugged, dry land with no villages would be a place of very few _____.

7. Why was the wilderness a land without borders?

8. Dr. Beck's general statement, which becomes his seventh trait, is that the wilderness lacks everything. Review the first six traits to remind yourself why the seventh is true. Read Jeremiah 2:6 to get the prophet's concept of wilderness. Which of Dr. Beck's traits are mentioned in this verse?

——————————— Episode 2 ———————————

HOW DOES GOD USE WILDERNESS?

Additional Reading: *Land without Borders* chapter 4, "How Does God Use Wilderness?"

Scripture Connection: Deuteronomy 8:2–3

PROLOGUE

While we may never have visited an actual wilderness territory, we certainly face wilderness times when we struggle. Dr. John Beck explains in this session of *Land without Borders* that God uses this kind of metaphor in teaching us about life's hard times. To do that, he takes his class (and us) to the Wilderness of Zin.

LOOKING BACK ON THE JOURNEY

Questions for consideration and discussion

1. If you have a chance, examine at a map of Israel in Bible times (with an atlas or online) and take a closer look at where the Wilderness of Zin is located. Is there anything about its location in relation to the Promised Land that surprises you?

2. Have you ever considered how short the quickest distance from Egypt to the Promised Land actually is? As Dr. Beck mentions, "Every expectation is that they would, as quickly as possible, move back to Canaan." Some say that if the Israelites had gone north, as Dr. Beck suggested, it would have taken them about two weeks to get back to the Promised Land. How does

that reality give you a new appreciation for why God instead extended their journey to forty years?

3. Reread Deuteronomy 8:2–3. Notice that the author of Deuteronomy mentions all three of the main ways, according to Dr. Beck, that God uses wilderness in our lives. What again are those three things?

4. According to Dr. Beck, "God hates arrogance." Can you think of some biblical stories in which God's disdain for arrogance is demonstrated?

5. Think of the comparison Dr. Beck makes between Egypt, where the Israelites resided for four hundred years, and the wilderness, where God sent them to learn more about Him. What about Egypt suggests that it is ripe for arrogance? And what does the wilderness teach, by contrast?

6. Just as the wilderness led to the God-directed question, "Do you trust me?" in the midst of this barrenness, how does a real-life

wilderness experience (trouble in our lives) cause us to ask the same question? What are some of the reasons we can answer "yes" to this question in our wilderness episodes of life?

7. While we don't often face hunger as the Israelites did in the desert—a hunger that was satisfied with God's supernatural gift of manna—we may face other times when we wait for God's provision and learn that He is sufficient. How has that happened in your life?

-------- Episode 3 --------

WILDERNESS AND FAITH WITNESS

Additional Reading: *Land without Borders* chapter 5, "Wilderness and Faith Witness"

Scripture Connection: 1 Samuel 24:1

PROLOGUE

Doesn't the word "oasis" sound somewhat exotic? Maybe it's because we've seen beautiful examples of this refreshing water source in movies. Or maybe just because we understand how exciting it must be for thirsty travelers to arrive at a place where cool spring water can restore their weary bodies. But regardless, we know that finding an oasis is a significant event. And, as Dr. John Beck explains, an oasis played a key role in the life of one of the Bible's most remarkable characters: David.

LOOKING BACK ON THE JOURNEY

Questions for consideration and discussion

1. Did you enjoy Dr. Beck's explanation of the water system in relation to the watershed line? How does that explain why there is an oasis where Dr. Beck and his students are located?

2. Why do you think God allowed Saul to so relentlessly chase the eventual king of Israel, David?

3. The En Gedi area was where David went to hide from Saul. Saul took 3,000 men with him, but there was probably only one place he would go where his men would not go to protect him. What was that one vulnerable situation, and what surprising event happened when Saul thought he was alone? Think about whether this was coincidence or God's guidance.

4. What do we learn about David and his relationship with God through this incident?

5. Imagine if we were to live so someone could say about us as Saul said to David, "You are more righteous than I." What experiences—even wilderness experiences—can we use to have such a faith witness?

6. Dr. Beck said the wilderness was reshaping David. How can we make sure our tough times reshape us into the kind of people God wants us to be?

──────────────── Episode 4 ────────────────

WILDERNESS WITHOUT WANTING

Additional Reading: *Land without Borders* chapter 6, "Wilderness without Wanting"

Scripture Connection: Psalm 23

PROLOGUE

Psalm 23. Majestic. Calming. Divine. Those words describing this much-loved passage—among the greatest pieces of literature ever written—don't sound like what we would recognize as related to the wilderness. But as Dr. John Beck explains in our fourth session of the *Land without Borders* study, Psalm 23 is a special kind of wilderness narrative—one that, when seen rightly, does indeed connect with the wilderness.

LOOKING BACK ON THE JOURNEY

Questions for consideration and discussion

1. What are some previous connections you have had with Psalm 23? In what ways has it calmed your heart or brought peace to your troubled soul?

2. What was your first thought when you heard Dr. Beck say that Psalm 23 should be placed in the context of wilderness? Did that surprise you? Did it cause you to quickly think through the passage in your mind to see how this could be true?

3. As has been mentioned, Psalm 23 is powerful. Think about the prospect, as Dr. Beck says, that when it is placed in its proper context of wilderness, "the language becomes even more powerful than it had been before." Were you skeptical about that assertion, or were you excited about what this might mean for you?

4. Was it a new idea for you that in biblical days, sheep and shepherds had to move into the fringes of the wilderness during crop-growing season? What is the standard picture you had of where sheep and their shepherds would hang out during the day?

5. "The Lord is my shepherd, I just don't lack a thing," Dr. Beck paraphrases Psalm 23:1. David saw his relationship with the Lord reflected in his flock's relationship with him. They lacked nothing as David lacked nothing. Are you feeling more or less like David at this moment in your life? Why?

6. Dr. Beck points out that just as a good shepherd leads his sheep over the rugged terrain of the wilderness safely, our good Shepherd "is always picking the right way to go." How is that true for us as we traverse our somewhat dangerous and rocky journey of life?

7. The psalm begins in the wilderness, Dr. Beck observes. However, it does not end in the wilderness. It ends, he says, "at home." Think about the contrast of life on earth (wilderness) and the life God has promised us (heaven). What comfort and hope does it promise you that, at the end, our Shepherd leads us home?

————————— Episode 5 —————————

WILDERNESS AND FORGIVENESS

Additional Reading: *Land without Borders* chapter 7, "Wilderness and Forgiveness"

Scripture Connection: Matthew 4:1–11; Deuteronomy 8:3

PROLOGUE

Had you ever thought to connect the story of Jesus's temptation by Satan in the wilderness to the Old Testament story of God's people, the Jews, while they were in the wilderness? If not, you'll be in for an interesting new concept as Dr. John Beck takes you and his students back into the Judean wilderness to make that connection. And you'll see how the idea of forgiveness is also clearly related to this wilderness incident.

LOOKING BACK ON THE JOURNEY

Questions for consideration and discussion

1. Dr. Beck walked his small cadre of students deep into the wilderness for this teaching segment. He did so to give them a glimpse of what the wilderness can do to a human—and to have them think about how it must have affected Jesus. Think through real-life symptoms Jesus must have felt while being in their barren landscape for forty days without food.

2. After reading Jesus's quote of Deuteronomy 8:3, Dr. Beck suggests that Matthew (who told this story of Jesus in the wilderness in

Matthew 4:1–4) has a strategy in mind. What is that strategy, and what is your first reaction to hearing about it?

3. Dr. Beck then details parallels that he suggests occur between the two stories: Jesus's temptation story and the children of Israel in the wilderness. He suggests, for instance, the parallel that God led both the Israelites and Jesus into the wilderness. And in doing so, He was asking them, "Do you trust me?" What are some wilderness times you have experienced in which God was asking you, "Do you trust me?" How did you do in those trials?

4. What Jesus did in the wilderness, according to Dr. Beck, is a picture of His putting salvation into action. "We see Him living out the obedience we and Israel owe the heavenly Father, but we couldn't deliver," he explained. "We know that Jesus has already succeeded on our behalf." How did Jesus meet the temptation Satan offered Him, and what does that tell us about how we should battle temptation?

5. "Jesus lived the life I couldn't so that I can walk out of here forgiven," Dr. Beck concludes. What are some of the ways you are thankful for the forgiveness that Jesus so freely offers us?

──────────── Episode 6 ────────────

WILDERNESS AND EXTRAVAGANT LOVE FOR OUR NEIGHBOR

Additional Reading: *Land without Borders* chapter 8, "Wilderness and Extravagant Love for Our Neighbor"

Scripture Connection: Luke 10:30

PROLOGUE

You can assume that most people have heard something about the story of the Good Samaritan. That term itself is part of both religious and secular vocabulary. But you may not know that this is a wilderness travel story. In the final trip into the wilderness for Dr. John Beck and his intrepid students, we'll discover what this wilderness travel story teaches us about demonstrating inconvenient, extravagant love to others.

LOOKING BACK ON THE JOURNEY

Questions for consideration and discussion

1. The story of the Good Samaritan is directly related to the wilderness because the incident Jesus told about in Luke 10:30 took place on a narrow road that meandered through the Judean wilderness. That road went from Jericho to Jerusalem. What difference does it make to you to realize that the story took place on a specific road going through a specific geographic place?

2. At the outset, Dr. Beck mentioned that there were some built-in animosities between Samaritans and Jews back in the day when this story was told. This sets up the tension in the moment the Samaritan comes up to the Jewish man who had been left for dead. Explain what the Samaritan did to show inconvenient, extravagant love to the injured man.

3. Dr. Beck goes on to explain some of the other dangers that a traveler would encounter on road—dangers that make the fact that the Good Samaritan stopped even more surprising. What were some additional dangers that might have made stopping more of a risk?

4. Loving our neighbors is one thing, but the Good Samaritan story, Dr. Beck says, sets up a totally different view of how we interact with our neighbors who are going through tough times—who are going through the wilderness. Think back on someone who was going through tough times. Was their situation handled with the same inconvenient, extravagant love the Samaritan showed toward the Jew? What new ways to think about helping your neighbors have you gained from listening to Dr. Beck in this session?

5. Dr. Beck closes by asking his students to allow the message of the wilderness to move from text to ground to heart. As you think back to these six lessons taught in the barren wilderness, which ones do you most desire to move from text to ground to heart for yourself?

Enjoy this book? Help us get the word out!

Share a link to the book or
mention it on social media

Write a review on your blog, on a retailer site,
or on our website (dhp.org)

Pick up another copy to share with someone

Recommend this book for your
church, book club, or small group

Follow Discovery House on
social media and join the discussion

Contact us to share your thoughts:

 @discoveryhouse    @DiscoveryHouse

Discovery House
P.O. Box 3566
Grand Rapids, MI 49501 USA

Phone: 1-800-653-8333
Email: books@dhp.org
Web: dhp.org